SHROPSHIRE PARISH
CHURCHES

SHROPSHIRE PARISH
CHURCHES

by John Leonard

With a foreword by
the Rt. Revd. Keith Sutton, Bishop of Lichfield,
and the Rt. Revd. John Oliver, Bishop of Hereford

The Breedon Books
Publishing Company
Derby

First published in Great Britain by
The Breedon Books Publishing Company Limited
44 Friar Gate, Derby, DE1 1DA
1994

For Richard

All royalties from the sale of this book will go to the
Church Urban Funds of the dioceses of Lichfield and
Hereford.

ISBN 1 873626 66 5

Printed and bound by Hillman Printers, Frome, Somerset
Covers printed by BDC Printing Services Limited of Derby

Contents

Foreword

Years ago in London, one of us met a young Dutch actor who was devoting his dramatic talents to Christian mission in the great city. When asked how he had come to faith, he said that it was through an experience of God's presence while sitting one day, as a student, in the impressive church of the Sacré Coeur in Paris.

The beauty of a church building can become a trigger of faith, and throughout this glorious county of Shropshire, our churches are living symbols of the precious nature of that Christian faith in God – tested by many centuries and found trustworthy by many generations.

Our hope is that anybody who takes up Dr. Leonard's sensitive record of these glorious buildings may be able, on occasion, to join with our people at their times of worship. For then the words of a distinguished modern historian may come true: "In an ancient church, the power of sacred association penetrates deeply into human hearts, kindling a sense of mystery, fortifying decisions of conscience and kindling hopes of eternity" (Owen Chadwick).

To anyone who takes up this lovely book, we wish you not only the pleasure of visiting a beautiful and historic building, but also the joy and consolation of living faith.

JOHN OLIVER, Bishop of Hereford
KEITH SUTTON, Bishop of Lichfield

Acknowledgements

Many people have helped in the production of this work. Once again, I have to thank Mrs J. Morgan, of Photoworld, Altrincham, Cheshire, for developing all the black-and-white photographs. I also thank English heritage for permission to quote their description of Langley Chapel; and BBC Enterprises Ltd for permission to quote from Richard Foster's Discovering English Churches. The incumbents of many of the churches illustrated have most generously given of their time and knowledge. Finally I must thank my wife and sons for their oft-tested patience and endurance in searching out old churches in Shropshire and elsewhere.

Introduction

SHROPSHIRE is still regarded by most people as primarily an agricultural county, though increasingly affected by pockets of industry. Away from these, the landscape remains glorious, especially perhaps in the southern uplands. In this landscape, and as an integral part of it, are over 200 parish churches of medieval foundation. They do not dominate the scene; towers or spires that can be seen for miles around are infrequent. But in their humble and unobtrusive way, they and the faith to which they bear witness have moulded for centuries the lives of the people. And their unostentatious character conceals riches of art, architecture and history which may often go unnoticed unless especially sought.

In this small volume, I describe the history of the church in Shropshire, sometimes relating this to the wider history of England and Wales. Then I draw attention to some of the special treasures which may be found, sometimes in the most unlikely cir-cumstances. And finally, 54 churches are described and illustrated in greater detail in the hope of encouraging more people to explore the wonders of past ages.

People who love visiting country churches have not many texts to guide them in Shropshire. The standard work is by Dean Cranage, and was written between 1894 and 1912. It is marvellously comprehensive, but quite unsuitable for taking on a visit to a country church – quite apart from the fact that it is almost unobtainable. Nikolaus Pevsner's *Shropshire* in *The Buildings of England* series is most useful for an account of the architecture, but perhaps does not really guide the non-expert to the most rewarding churches.

I trust that the present volume will do this, and will prove of value both to those fortunate enough to live in the county, and to those many visitors who love Shropshire and come, often repeatedly, to explore its towns and countryside.

By the same author: *Derbyshire Parish Churches*.

The Development of the Church In Shropshire

IN THE seventeenth century, Thomas Fuller (in Fuller's Worthies) described Shropshire as 'a large and lovely county generally fair and fruitful, affording grass, grain and all things necessary for man's sustenance'. It was not always thus. In ancient times, Shropshire was heavily wooded and settlements were sparse, probably being most evident along the Severn valley. The Romans came and established their base at Wroxeter (Viroconium), and at one time this was the fourth largest town in Roman Britain. The centuries following their departure (around AD 400) are shrouded in uncertainty, and it is not until the seventh century that reliable historical records are resumed. Then the northern part of the county came to be part of the petty kingdom of the Wroecensaetan, while the southern part was conquered by the Mercians under their king Penda in 628. In 641, Penda defeated and slew the Christian King Oswald of Northumbria at the battle of Maserfelt; the site was later called Oswestry (St Oswald's Tree) by the Normans. Penda established the kingdom of the Magonsaetan in south Shropshire and Herefordshire. It is said that the boundary between the Magonsaetan and the Wroecensaetan still demarcates the limits of the dioceses of Lichfield and Hereford in Shropshire. In 655, Penda was slain in battle by Oswald's brother Oswy; his son and heir Peada was converted to Christianity, and the formal conversion of Mercia rapidly followed – Mercia was the last of the Anglo-Saxon kingdoms to embrace the faith. Chad (Ceadda) the first bishop of Mercia, was consecrated in 669 and fixed his see at Lichfield.

The first Christian foundation in Shropshire of which we have any record is the convent for monks and nuns established at Wenlock in 680. Originally, Wenlock was a daughter establishment to the monastery at Icanhoe (usually identified as Boston in Lincolnshire) founded by St Botolf. The site was given by Merewalh, another son of Penda, who was the king of the Magonsaetan, and his daughter Mildburge became the first abbess. She was later canonised, and her name survives in the area in Stoke St Milborough. Wenlock was granted extensive estates in Shropshire, especially around the Clee Hills and in Corvedale, and also in Wales.

Eventually the whole of the county became part of the kingdom of Mercia, which reached its pinnacle of power under kings Aethelbald and Offa in the eighth century. As elsewhere in Saxon England, the organisation of the church was relatively loose. Originally, a number of minsters arose, usually serving a very wide area, and being staffed by a variable number of canons; these are the Saxon collegiate churches referred to later. In the later Saxon centuries, many village churches were founded by laymen, with only a tenuous relationship with the local bishop. These churches were often regarded by the local thane as part of his personal property, almost as a capital investment; for ownership of a church increasingly brought in revenue in the form of tithes. Thus the large areas served by the older minsters became progressively subdivided as parishes multiplied.

In Shropshire, an unknown number of Saxon churches were built; the great majority of these were of timber, and so have not survived. The use of stone for the construction of parish churches was most unusual before c.950. There were, however, exceptions: at Wroxeter, for example, the adjacent Roman ruins provided a ready source for stone, and the north wall of the church has been dated to the seventh or eighth century. At Barrow, also, the chancel has been ascribed to the eighth century. By the eleventh century stone was being used increasingly, and the nave and north transept at Stanton Lacy is a fine example of work from this period.

There are a number of characteristic features which identify Saxon stonework. At corners, slabs were often set alternately vertically and horizontally – long-and-short work – a feature not found in Norman building. In the north wall at Wroxeter, traces of long-and-short work can be discerned at the junction between the Saxon and Norman portions (Fig.1). Herring-bone masonry consists of rows of stones applied diagonally, each row leaning alternately to the right and the left. Saxon masonry of this type may be seen at Diddlebury (Fig.2) and possibly at Rushbury, while in early Norman building it may been seen at Clee St Margaret, Culmington, Pitchford, Sidbury and

(Fig 1) **St Andrew, Wroxeter** *North wall of nave. Between the two windows is the demarcation between the Saxon building on the left and thirteenth-century building on the right. Traces of long-and-short work may be discerned in the Saxon masonry at the boundary.*

(Fig 2) **St Peter, Diddlebury** *Herring-bone masonry and Saxon window in the north wall of the nave.*

(Fig 4) **St Peter, Diddlebury** *Saxon doorway.*

(Fig 3) **St Peter, Stanton Lacy** *Pilaster strips and Saxon doorway.*

Stanton-upon-Hine-Heath. Finally, for decoration, very typical Saxon features are tall, thin strips or pilasters – thin flat stones applied vertically – best seen in Shropshire at Stanton Lacy (Fig.3). Saxon windows are small, usually high up, and sometimes splayed equally both inside and outside (Norman windows are splayed internally). They may be round-headed or triangular-headed, the former being seen at Barrow and Diddlebury (Fig.2). Saxon doorways are plain (Figs 3 and 4).

The arrival of William the Conqueror in 1066 swept away Saxon England, and the Normans introduced their own style of so-called Romanesque architecture. But this did not happen overnight and buildings dating from the last 30 years of the eleventh century often show features of both Saxon and Norman influence, making it difficult, sometimes impossible, for experts to assign a date with any confidence. The fact is that Norman influence was making itself felt in England before 1066, and Saxon influence persisted after that watershed year. But from 1100 onwards, Saxon styles are extinguished.

There was an astonishing explosion of church building in Shropshire in the twelfth century, as in England as a whole. Over 100 churches in the county show unmistakable Norman features: in addition, an

(Fig 5) **St Mary, Cold Weston**

unknown number of Norman churches have either disappeared completely (where villages have withered away) or have been completely replaced by later buildings. It is probable that in the twelfth century at least 150 parish churches were built, an impressive record for a sparsely-populated impoverished county, remote from the power-centre of the country.

In the smallest Norman churches, there was just a nave and chancel, and this is to be seen in its purest form in Shropshire at Heath chapel – a perfectly preserved and virtually unaltered building for over 800 years. It stands alone in a field, the surrounding village having withered away over the centuries. The land around Brown Clee Hill was marginal for agricultural purposes, and life there must have been a perpetual struggle for existence and survival against adverse natural circumstances. Not only Heath village succumbed: Abdon and Cold Weston are other communities that have virtually disappeared. Where the population declined severely, the church was often allowed to fall into decay, and a number in Shropshire have disappeared without trace. This process can still be witnessed, for only two miles from Heath stands the isolated, but dilapidated, church at Cold Weston (Fig.5). Like Heath, the church stands alone in a field, with only one nearby cottage. The building is markedly inferior to Heath, and has none of the grace of the latter church so that it undoubtedly suffers by comparison, and also because of its proximity to Heath. At the time of writing (early 1991) it is intended to convert this building into a dwelling, and it is to be hoped that the minimum of alteration will be

allowed, and that the restoration will take place before irreversible decay has set in.

Where Norman churches were built in more prosperous areas – fortunately, the majority – they were usually enlarged to cater for the expanding population. This was done by lateral extension of the

(Fig 6) St **John the Baptist, Kinlet** *Norman arcade, with massive cylindrical piers and semicircular arches.*

nave in the form of aisles, separated from the nave by arcades of semicircular arches supported by massive cylindrical piers or columns (Fig.6). The piers are surmounted by square-edged capitals which effect the transition from the round column to the square abacus above which supports the arch (Fig.7). The inferior surface of the capital is often carved into a cushion (a rounding-off of the lower angles into the cylindrical shaft below), scallop (a further modification in which

(Fig 7) **St Mary, Shawbury** *Beneath the square abacus, the capital is carved with many small scallops.*

the surface is elaborated into a series of truncate cones) or volute (spiral scrolls – Fig.8).

Semicircular arches are also found above doorways and windows, and are of course, the hallmark of Norman architecture. They often became decorated by geometric designs, the commonest being the chevron or zig-

zag, which was introduced c.1120 (Fig.9). Other Norman ornamental motifs are beak-head (the repeated use of stylised heads of birds or mammals with long beaks), billet (short raised rectangles placed at regular intervals) and nail-head (small pyramids regularly repeated). Late in the Norman period, and continuing more typically

(Fig 10) **Holy Trinity, Wistantow** *South chancel doorway, showing dogtooth decoration.*

into the next century, dogtooth occurs (a series of four-cornered stars placed diagonally and raised pyramidally – Fig.10). Norman windows are usually small and round-headed, and are deeply splayed

(Fig 8) **Holy Trinity, Wheathill** *Norman chancel arch, with scroll capitals.*

(Fig 9) **St James, Stirchley** *Ornate Norman chancel arch, with three orders of voussoirs, the inner with chain-links, and the outer two with zigzag.*

(Fig 11) **St John the Baptist, Hope Bagot** *Interior view of the deeply splayed Norman window in the north wall of the chancel.*

internally (but not externally) to maximise the provision of light, glass being expensive (Fig.11).

Not content with parish-church building on such an impressive scale, the Normans also built a series of monasteries. We have seen that the earliest monastery in Shropshire was Wenlock, founded *c.*680. In the later Saxon centuries, this foundation fared badly, perhaps as a result of Danish raids, and it appears to have been re-founded by Leofric, Earl of Mercia during the reign of Edward the Confessor (1050). After the Norman Conquest, William I established Shropshire as a county Palatinate under his cousin, Roger de Montgomery; his territory extended west of Offa's Dyke into the upper Severn valley in Wales. Earl Roger founded Montgomery Castle, naming it after his family seat in Normandy (Rowley). He also built Shrewsbury Castle (1067-69), founded Shrewsbury Abbey (1083), and re-founded Wenlock Priory. He sent for monks from a leading Cluniac house at Charité-sur-Loire for Wenlock, and the priory acquired extensive properties in Shropshire. The Benedictine Abbey of St Peter and St Paul at Shrewsbury was founded as a daughter house of Seez in Normandy and was also endowed with much property.

Fifty years later, further abbeys were founded: Haughmond (1130), Buildwas (1135) and Lilleshall (1143). At Haughmond, the Augustinian Priory of St John the Evangelist was founded by William FitzAlan, and became an abbey five years later. Buildwas was founded by Roger de Clinton, bishop of Coventry and Lichfield, as a daughter house of Furness Abbey, for monks of the Savigniac order; later it became Cistercian (1147). The Augustinian abbey at Lilleshall was originally founded at Lizard in 1143 by Philip de Belmeis, but was re-founded five years later at Lilleshall by Philip's brother Richard,

who was dean of the collegiate church of St Alkmund, Shrewsbury.

Most of the Norman building in Shropshire was concentrated in the period 1150-1200; the best examples of earlier work being Shrewsbury Holy Cross (the original Shrewsbury Abbey, late eleventh century), and Heath and Morville (1100-1150). In the last forty years of the twelfth century, the gradual introduction of the Gothic style of pointed arch may be seen; where this occurs alongside Norman features, the style is known as Transitional (Fig.12). The introduction of the pointed arch, which was to revolutionise church architecture, was primarily for structural reasons, such an arch being able to transmit a larger proportion of the thrust directly to the ground (Foster). It appears to have been first used at Autun Cathedral, France, around 1120-30, but was not seen in England until about 1160. From then onwards, it was seen side by side with semicircular arches (the Transitional period) until after about 1200 semicircular arches are seen no more, and the Early English period is said to have begun.

The Early English style covers roughly the whole of the thirteenth century, and work of this period is frequently seen in Shropshire alongside earlier Norman architecture. The reason for this is that increasing prosperity and growing population required the progressive enlargement of many churches by the addition of aisles or the lengthening of naves and chancels. Although much Norman work was sound and has stood the test of time, some was less good and required replacement.

Replacement was not often wholesale, however, and this explains the rarity of pure Early English churches in Shropshire; the best are Acton Burnell and Longnor, and the cruciform church at Neen Sollars, all built towards the end of the century.

(Fig 12) **Aston Eyre** *The pointed chancel arch of the late Norman period (Transitional).*

(Fig 13) **St Mary, Cleobury Mortimer** *Early English piers surmounted by rounded capitals; the arches are acutely pointed.*

In Early English Churches, the semi-circular arches and thick cylindrical piers of the Norman age have given way to acutely-pointed arches supported by less substantial piers (Fig.13), often with fillets (thin longitudinal bands running

(Fig 14) **St Mary, Shrewsbury** *Early thirteenth-century capital carved with stiff-leaf foliage.*

down the shaft). The piers are now surmounted by capitals with a rounded (instead of a square) upper edge, and are characteristically decorated with 'stiff-leaf' foliage (Fig.14). The dogtooth pattern is also found in Early English arcades. Instead of the deeply recessed small Norman windows, tall lancet windows with acutely pointed upper ends are seen, often in groups of three at the east end of the church (Fig.15). Externally, lancet windows were provided with a hood-mould of projecting masonry to throw the rainwater clear of the window. Sometimes two or more lancets were enclosed by the same hood-mould to prevent the water from puddling between them; this necessarily also enclosed a small area of blank wall at the apex below the common hood-mould. Later in the century, this area was often pierced, resulting in plate or Y-tracery above the lancet windows (Fig.16). From this germ, the later development of complex tracery seen in the next century evolved.

(Fig 15) **St Edith, Eaton-Under-Haywood** *Lancet windows in east wall of chancel.*

(Fig 16) **St
Andrew, Shifnal**
*The twin lancet
windows of the
Early English
porch, with plate
tracery above.*

The Decorated style was introduced elsewhere in England around 1300, and arrived in Shropshire somewhat later; the most complete example in the county is probably at Chelmarsh. Decorated arches are not so acutely pointed as in the preceding period, and the piers are more often octagonal than circular in cross-section (Fig.17). The carvings on the moulded capitals are fewer and more elaborate, and when foliage is seen it is more realistic than the stiff-leaf carving of the Early English style. But the most characteristic feature of the Decorated style, which was to stamp its hallmark on the whole fourteenth century, was the ogee arch – two shallow, S-shaped curves meeting upwards in a sharp point, and often embellished with crockets and other ornamental features (Fig.18). There was nothing functional about the ogee arch – it was an exuberant artistic fancy. In windows it led to complicated patterns of flowing tracery (Figs. 19 and 20), some of which may be described as geometrical, curvilinear or reticulated.

(Fig 17) **St Michael, Lilleshall** *Decorated arcade (less acutely pointed than in the Early English style) supported by octagonal piers.*

(Fig 18) **St Mary, Acton Burnell** *Decorated recess with ogee top.*

Left: (Fig 19) **St Michael, Munslow** *Early fourteenth-century (Decorated) window in the north aisle.*

Below: (Fig 20) **St Mary Magdalene, Albrighton (near Shifnal)** *A complex pattern of Decorated tracery in the east window of the chancel.*

Striking examples of such windows may be seen at Shifnal and Kinlet. Another characteristic motif of the Decorated age was ball-flower ornamentation – a small ball enclosed by three petals forming a globular flower (Fig.21); this was often set in rows on a concave moulding on windows and elsewhere.

Bubonic plague struck England in 1348-50, and the Black Death wiped out a quarter, perhaps a third, of the population. It is a tribute to the faith in medieval times that, in this ghastly fourteenth century, when plague was compounded by bad harvests and disaster occurred on a scale never known in England before or since, there was no pause in church building in many counties. In Cheshire, for example, there was a notable surge of building between 1350 and 1400, and later, in the fifteenth century, all the noblest medieval churches in Cheshire were completed (Nantwich, Bunbury, Astbury, Malpas, Great Budworth). In Shropshire, however, Perpendicular churches are not frequent. There is, of course, the gorgeous and spectacular church of St Laurence in Ludlow, and the two richly-endowed collegiate churches of Battlefield and Tong. Of village churches, the best in the style are Ightfield and Edgmond. As will be noted later, however, there are about 27 Perpendicular towers in the county attached to churches of earlier construction. It seems that in Shropshire, compared with many other counties, tower-building alone in the Perpendicular age was all that was required or could be afforded. It is difficult to avoid the conclusion that the county in the later fourteenth and fifteenth centuries was relatively poor, with a population that was not expanding. Certainly, apart from Ludlow, nothing approaching the grand Perpendicular churches built elsewhere in England can be found.

The Perpendicular style prevailed in England for 200 years (*c*.1350-1550), persisting until the Reformation. The emphasis throughout is on

Right: (Fig 21) **St Peter, Chelmarsh** *Ball-flower ornamentation on a capital.*

Below: (Fig 22) **St Peter, Edgmond** *Perpendicular arcade.*

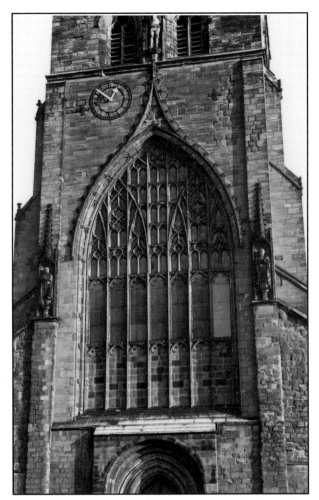

(Fig 23) **Holy Cross, Shrewsbury** *The finest Perpendicular window in Shropshire.*

verticality; straight lines replace the sinuous tracery of the Decorated period; the pointed arches become flatter (Fig.22). This 'alters the proportions of the arcade: a larger part of its height is now taken up by the piers. The piers being both taller and thinner make the arcade appear loftier and produce the impression of height and lightness of structure that is so characteristic of the Perpendicular style. The effect is enhanced by the addition of the clerestory, now almost a routine feature of the parish church . . .The preference for straight lines shows particularly clearly in window tracery. There the vertical mullions that divide a window into its lights rise almost without interruption to the head of the window, ruling its tracery into tiers of rectangular compartments.' (Foster, p161) (Fig.23).

The building of churches came to an abrupt end, in Shropshire, as elsewhere in England, with the Reformation, but there is one notable exception. Langley chapel was built in the reign of Queen Elizabeth, and though now disused, it remains a moving memorial to the simplicities of Puritan worship (p75). In the seventeenth century, a number of churches were built: Loughton (1622), simple and small (Fig.24); Stokesay (1654) rebuilt after severe damage in the Civil War; Berwick (1672, Fig.25) and Minsterley (1689) being good examples of this period. A number of adaptations and alterations to earlier churches were made, notably Adderley, High Ercall, Lydham and Oswestry.

With the eighteenth century, classical forms came into their own, and quite the best early eighteenth-century church in Shropshire is Whitchurch (1712). A large number of very ordinary village churches were built, especially in the north of the county. In the last decade of the century came St Chad's Shrewsbury, St Mary Magdalene's Bridgnorth, and St Michael's Madeley, the last two being designed by Thomas Telford.

From the sixteenth century onwards, the imparkation of land around manor houses resulted in the establishment of a number of 'estate churches'. A number of great families, building or rebuilding their stately homes, wished not to have the hovels of the poor on their doorstep, and ruthlessly removed the inhabitants to a more discreet location out of sight of the hall. The result now is that the medieval parish

(Fig 24) **Loughton** *An early seventeenth-century church.*

(Fig 25) **Berwick** *A late seventeenth-century church adjacent to Berwick House.*

church remains adjacent to the great house and remote from the village. Such a setting is now often very attractive, though the arrangement must be highly inconvenient to the parishioners. Churches of this kind may be seen at Upton Cressett, Acton Burnell, Moreton Corbet and above all at Kinlet.

Victorian churches exist in abundance in Shropshire, but are largely outside the scope of this work. In the pages that follow I have included just two: Llanyblodwel, because it is a charming mid-nineteenth-century adaptation of an earlier building in a lovely setting; and Batchcott (Richard's Castle) built in 1891-2, and designed by Norman Shaw – an outstanding example of Victorian architecture.

Stonework and Woodwork in Shropshire Churches

LTHOUGH the quality of medieval carving in Shropshire may not equal that seen, say, in Herefordshire, nevertheless there is much remarkable work to admire. The Herefordshire School originated in the mid-twelfth century, and their work may be seen at Kilpeck, Fownhope, Castle Frome and elsewhere in that county. In Shropshire churches, their influence is clearest in the font at Stottesdon and the tympanum at Aston Eyre.

Fonts

There are a large number of medieval or earlier fonts in Shropshire – Cranage counted 130. Those at Wroxeter (Fig.77, p32) and Shrewsbury Holy Cross, and the base of that at Woolstaston (Fig.26), are apparently of Roman origin, and that at Bucknell (Fig.27) may be Anglo-Saxon. By common consent, the finest Norman font is at Stottesdon (Fig.102, p40). Other notable Norman fonts may be seen at Adderley, Berrington, Claverley, Edgmond, Holdgate, Linley,

(Fig 26) **St Michael, Woolstaston** *Double font: the upper bowl is Norman, the lower possibly Roman.*

Morville, Shawbury and Upton Cressett. The fonts at Adderley and Berrington are illustrated here (Figs. 28 and 29), the remainder being shown later in the book, under the entries of their respective churches. The Early English font at Acton Burnell (Fig.169, p64) and the Perpendicular one at Munslow (Fig.30) are also excellent.

(Fig 27) **St Mary, Bucknell** *Font, probably Saxon.*

(Fig 28) **St Peter, Adderley** *Norman font.*

(Fig 29) **All Saints, Berrington** *Norman font.*

Tympana

The tympanum is the space between the lintel of a doorway and the arch above it, and this area was sometimes filled with sculpted designs. The earliest is probably at Barrow (Fig.31), dating from the late eleventh century; those at Uppington (Fig.32) and Stottesdon (Fig.33) are also probably of this time. At Barrow, the tympanum is carved with various geometrical patterns, while at Uppington, there is rather crudely carved dragon work. At Stottesdon there is a bearded head at the apex of the triangle, with a pattern of crosses on the tympanum and beasts on the lintel. At High Ercall, a remarkable early Norman tympanum is set in the north wall of the nave (Fig. 34); this represents the Tree of Life, and has been dated by Gethyn-Jones to

Right: (Fig 30) **St Michael, Munslow** *Perpendicular font.*

Below: (Fig 31) **St Giles, Barrow** *Late eleventh-century tympanum.*

Right, top: (Fig 32) **Holy Trinity, Uppington** *Late eleventh-century tympanum.*

Right, middle: (Fig 33) **St Mary, Stottesdon** *Late eleventh-century tympanum.*

Right, bottom: (Fig 34) **St Michael, High Ercall** *Early twelfth-century tympanum.*

(Fig 35) **Aston Eyre** *Mid-twelfth-century tympanum; the finest Norman carving in Shropshire.*

*c.*1110-15. The mid-twelfth-century carving at Aston Eyre (Fig.35) is the finest: an exquisite representation of the Entry into Jerusalem, with Christ riding on an ass, flanked on the right by an older man spreading palm leaves and on the left by a young man with an ass.

Monuments

A rich assembly of monuments may be seen in Shropshire churches: brasses at Acton Burnell, Burford, Ightfield and Ludford (Fig.36), wooden effigies at Berrington, Eaton-under-Haywood and Pitchford, and incised slabs at Claverley (Fig.37) and Pitchford. These, however, are eclipsed by the magnificent series of alabaster and stone effigies at Tong (Figs.187-9, pp 69, 70), which are of national importance. It is impossible to illustrate more than a small proportion of the other fine monuments; here are shown examples from Lilleshall, Norton-in-Hales, Neen Sollars, and Acton Round (Figs.38-41) and in the following pages monuments at Acton Burnell, Claverley, Condover, Kinlet, Moreton Corbet, Moreton Say, Wroxeter and elsewhere are shown.

Roofs

The Shropshire churches have a great variety of roof construction. The oldest form, dating from the Norman period, is the trussed-rafter roof, the earliest

(Fig 36) **St Giles, Ludford** *Brass of William Fox and his wife (1554).*

(Fig 38) **St Michael, Lilleshall** *Monument to Sir Richard (died 1661)
and Lady (died 1674) Leveson.*

(Fig 37) **All Saints, Claverley** *Incised slab in memory of Francis and
Elizabeth Gatacre (1599).*

(Fig 39) **St Chad, Norton-In-Hales** *Monument to Sir Rowland and Lady Francis Cotton. Lady Cotton died in childbirth in 1606.*

(Fig 40) **All Saints, Neen Sollars** *Monument to Humfrey Conyngesby (1624).*

(Fig 41) **Acton Round** *Monument to Sir Whitmore and Lady Acton. Designed by T.F.Pritchard, c.1760.*

Right: (Fig 42)
Longnor
Trussed-rafter roof.

Below: (Fig 43)
St Michael, Onibury *Tie-beam roof.*

surviving example probably being at Wistanstow (ascribed by Cranage to the thirteenth century). Other medieval trussed-rafter roofs survive at Church Stretton, Kinlet, Longnor (Fig.42), Neen Sollars and

Above: (Fig 44) **St Mary, Neen Savage** *Heavy tie-beams span the nave, with trussed rafters above.*

Left: (Fig 45) **St Eata, Atcham** *Tie-beams span the chancel, with collar-beams and arched braces above and over the nave.*

Stottesdon. In this type, each pair of common rafters is supported by struts, and just below the ridge they are bound together by a short horizontal collar-beam; sometimes intersecting beams were placed diagonally between opposite rafters (scissor-beams) in addition to, or instead of, collar-beams (Foster).

Tie-beam roofs were also developed in the twelfth century. 'Hefty timbers, the tie-beams, were laid across from wall to wall. On their ends rested the bottoms of the main rafters, the principals, which met at the roof ridge. The principals were given extra support by a central king-post. The king-post rested on the tie-beam and sometimes branched into two or more struts at the top. Instead of a king-post a pair of shorter queen-posts might be used on either side of the centre. This braced triangular shape formed the basic truss of the roof. Between these trusses ran the longitudinal members: the ridge at the top, the wall-plates directly on top of the walls, and halfway between, the purlins which carried the sloping common rafters. The heavy tie-beams were very prone to sagging in the middle and were often cambered (given a slight upward curve) to counteract this tendency and given support underneath by a pair of arch-braces curving down to wall-posts, which were

Above: (Fig 46) **St Mary Magdalene, Albrighton (near Shifnal)** *Collar-beam roof.*

Right: (Fig 47) **Holy Trinity, Lydham** *Nave roof showing one tie-beam, collar-beams on arched braces, with wind-braces forming quatrefoil patterns on each side.*

Above: (Fig 48) **St Edith, Eaton-under-Haywood** *Low-pitched roof of the chancel, with decorative bosses. A tie-beam spans the nave.*

(Fig 49) **St Mary, Shrewsbury** *Low-pitched tie-beam roof, with arched braces, decorative bosses, and cusped quatrefoils in the panels.*

in turn supported by stone corbels bonded into the nave walls.' (Foster). Tie-beam roofs may be seen at Atcham (Fig.45), Eaton-under-Haywood (Fig.48), Ightfield, Onibury (Fig.43), Neen Savage (Fig.44), and Quatt.

Later in the medieval period, the arch-braced roof was developed. Instead of a tie-beam 'the principals were supported by continuously curved arch-braces which sprang from wall-posts to prevent the roof from spreading outwards. The arch-braces were tied together towards the top of the roof by a collar-beam, so they acted, in effect, as a wooden arch supporting the principals.' (Foster). Cranage estimated that there are nearly 100 collar-braced roofs in the county, and especially in the west wind-braces were added on each side to support the purlins; these were often cusped to form quatrefoil patterns. The best example is at Alberbury, but they may also be seen at Albrighton near Shifnal (Fig.46), Clun, Hopesay and Lydham (Fig.47).

Lead was readily available in medieval England, and gradually replaced thatching or wooden shingles for roofing. This led to a reduction in the steepness of slope of the roof, to avoid the tendency of the lead to slide down the slope. This enabled the nave and aisles to be roofed separately, thus clearing the way for clerestories with taller windows. Roofs of low pitch were developed, and frequently panelling appeared

between the beams, with carved bosses at the intersections. These may be seen at the chancel at Eaton-under-Haywood (Fig.15, p13, and Fig.48), the

(Fig 50) **All Saints, Claverley** *Another low-pitched tie-beam roof, with extra embellishment forming a ceilure above the rood.*

Right: (Fig 51) **St Mary Magdalene, Battlefield** *Nineteenth-century hammer-beam roof.*

Below: (Fig 52) **St Cuthbert, Donington** *Seventeenth-century double hammer-beam roof.*

Left: (Fig 53) **St George, Milson** *Elizabethan pulpit.*

Below: (Fig 54) **Middleton (near Ludlow)** *A Victorian reconstruction of a medieval rood-screen and loft.*

south chapel at Ellesmere and above all at the nave at Shrewsbury St Mary (Fig.49). An unusual feature at Claverley is the extra embellishment over the former site of the rood screen forming a ceilure (Fig.50).

In the sixteenth and seventeenth centuries, hammer-beam roofs were introduced, though much earlier examples may be found outside Shropshire. 'The practical virtue . . .was that it enabled the roof to cover a wider span by eliminating the heavy tie-beams, which were always prone to sag; . . .The tie-beam was replaced by a pair of . . .hammer-like brackets which rest on top of the wall and project several feet into the nave with the help of supporting wall-posts and arch-braces. On the hammer-beams stand the struts or arch-braces which in turn support the principal rafters of the roof.' (Foster). The finest hammer-beam roof spans the very wide nave at

Condover (Fig.205, p76); others may be seen at Battlefield (Fig.51), Donington (Fig.52), High Ercall and Shifnal (Fig.166, p62).

Pulpits, stalls and pews

The only medieval pulpit in a Shropshire church is at Onibury (Fig.109, p42), and there is an Elizabethan one at Milson (Fig.53). Of the numerous seventeenth-century pulpits, Cleobury North, Clun (Fig.156, p59) Lydbury North, Quatt, Shawbury, Tong and Wroxeter date from the reigns of James I or Charles I; fine canopied post-Restoration pulpits may be seen at Eaton-under-Haywood (1670) and Minsterley (1689). Late Georgian three-decker pulpits are at St Martin's (Fig.154, p58) and Ashford Bowdler.

Medieval choir-stalls and misericords may be seen at Ludlow and Tong (q.v.). The finest screen in Shropshire is at Hughley (Figs.173-6, p65); other good screens are at Neen Savage (Fig.158, p60), and Bettws-y-Crwyn. At Middleton, near Ludlow, a rood-

(Fig 55) **All Saints, Worthen** *Box-pews and benches.*

(Fig 56) **St Peter and St Paul, Cleobury North** *Seventeenth-century pew.*

(Fig 57) **St Mary, Leebotwood** *Box-pews and west gallery.*

Right: (Fig 58) **St John the Baptist, Stokesay** *Canopied pew.*

screen with loft on coving has been erected partly using medieval woodwork (Fig.54). The finest set of box-pews are at Worthen (Fig.55), where there is also a rare series of medieval benches in the middle of the nave. Other furnishings of note are at Cleobury North (Fig.56), Heath, Holdgate, Langley, Leebotwood (Fig.57) and Stokesay (Fig.58).

Towers

To the world outside, the tower is the most obvious and accessible part of the village church, often visible for miles around. Shropshire towers are modest in comparison with those, say, of Somerset or East Anglia, but nevertheless they are a familiar and much-loved element in the village scene. About eighty-five towers remain from medieval times, spread fairly evenly from the twelfth to the sixteenth centuries. One difficulty in dating towers is that windows were often later inserted into an earlier structure: thus an Early English window may be found in a Norman tower, causing considerable confusion. Another difficulty in classification is that parts of some towers were built at widely different periods: the lower storeys might be Norman or Early English, and the belfry Perpendicular (e.g. Rushbury, Fig.62, Atcham, Fig.63). After taking these factors into consideration, Cranage classified the medieval towers as follows: twelfth century (Norman) 23; thirteenth century (Early English) 21; fourteenth century (Decorated) 14; fourteenth to sixteenth centuries (Perpendicular) 27. When one recalls that only a handful of Shropshire churches are mainly Perpendicular, it is obvious that there must be many churches in which a Perpendicular tower has been added to a much earlier structure (e.g. Wroxeter, Shawbury).

By far the commonest site for the tower is at the west end of the nave, and the ground floor of the tower usually opens into the nave through a tower arch. Of the 85 medieval towers in Shropshire, 65 (77 per cent) are western. Cruciform churches, with a central tower and transepts, are unusual in villages, but tend to occur more frequently in small towns; there are only nine in Shropshire (Church Stretton, Ellesmere, Ludlow, Neen Sollars, Shifnal, Stanton Lacy, Tong, Wistanstow, Wrockwardine). Four churches have a north or north-western tower (Alberbury, Bromfield, Hodnet and Worfield) and seven have a south, south-western or south-eastern tower (St Leonard Bridgnorth, Child's Ercall, Claverley, Cleobury North, Eaton-under-Haywood, Oswestry, and Worfield).

There are no Saxon towers in Shropshire, so the earliest structures date back to Norman times, squat, sturdy, plain, solidly-built, with thick walls. In the west of the county, it is possible that some may have been built partly to offer refuge to the people in times of border warfare (as in Northumberland). At belfry level, there are usually two round-headed windows divided by a shaft, with a larger round-headed arch surmounting both. The roof may be flat and plain, but can by pyramidal. Clun (Fig.59), Hopesay and More have a double-pyramid roof. Alberbury (Fig.172, p65) is unique in the county in having a gabled roof known as a saddleback. Buttresses in the twelfth century usually clasp the angles of the tower (e.g. Albrighton, Fig.61).

Early English towers have pointed lancet windows,

(Fig 59) **St George, Clun** *Norman tower.*

(Fig 60) **St Mary, Bromfield** *Early English tower, with Perpendicular battlements.*

(Fig 61) **St Mary Magdalene, Albrighton (near Shifnal)** *Norman tower, with an Early English lancet window and Perpendicular battlements.*

and the belfry windows become more prominent. Spires were developed but rarely in Shropshire; in broach-spires, semi-pyramidal pieces of masonry at the junction of the square top of the tower effected a smooth transition to the usually octagonal spire (e.g. Bitterley (Fig.68), and Cleobury Mortimer (Fig. 69). Buttresses in the thirteenth century were usually placed at each corner, at right-angles to each other (e.g. Bromfield, Fig.60). The projection of the buttresses diminishes towards the top of the tower, and was reduced stepwise with a sloping set-off to shed rainwater (e.g. Hodnet, Fig.64).

Decorated towers were typically of four storeys: the ground floor, opening into the nave through the tower arch; above this, a ringers' gallery, with small windows; then the belfry, with prominent windows; and at the top, the roof surmounted with a spire. The spire at Worfield (Fig.71) is the finest in the county and is recessed within a parapet, in contrast to the broach-spire. Buttressing in the fourteenth and later centuries was usually diagonal, placed at the four corners of the structure. The tower at Hodnet, octagonal from bottom to top, is unique in Shropshire (Fig.64).

In the Perpendicular period, towers are usually topped by a battlemented parapet, below which is often a decorative frieze (e.g. Cheswardine, Fig.65, Shawbury, Fig.66 and Ightfield, Fig.70). Parapets were developed when lead roofing was introduced and lowered the pitch of the roof. Previously, the roof was supported at the eaves by a corbel-table, overlapping it so that rainwater was thrown clear of the walls. When the roof became flatter, it ended in a gutter behind the parapet, and the water then escaped from the gutter through spouts (gargoyles) often fantastically carved into grotesque shapes, which project from the wall just below the parapet (Fig.70).

Towers from the eighteenth century are shown at Selattyn (Fig.67), Chelmarsh (Fig.177, p66), Whitchurch (Fig.208, p77), Quatt (Fig.210, p78) and Moreton Say (Fig.217, p80).

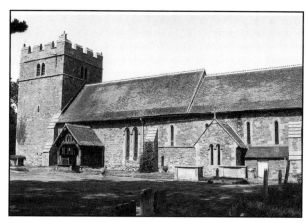

(Fig 62) **St Peter, Rushbury** *Early English tower, with Perpendicular battlements.*

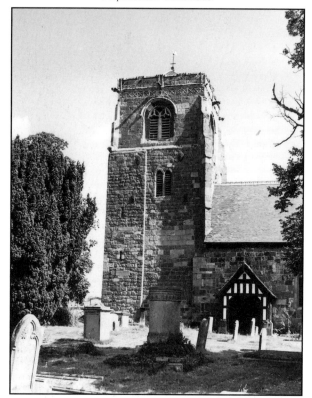

(Fig 63) **St Eata, Atcham** *Early English tower, with Perpendicular quatrefoil frieze and parapet above.*

(Fig 64) **St Luke, Hodnet** *Decorated octagonal tower.*

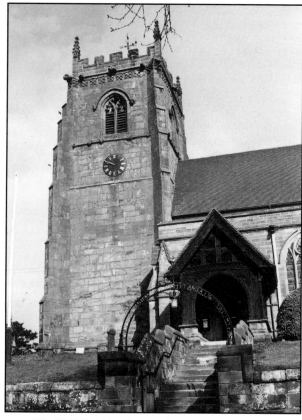

(Fig 65) **St Swithin, Cheswardine** *Perpendicular tower.*

(Fig 66) **St Mary, Shawbury** *Perpendicular tower.*

(Fig 67) **St Mary, Selattyn** *Tower built in 1703.*

Above: (Fig 68) **St Mary, Bitterley** *Early English tower, with timber-framed top and broach-spire.*

Left: (Fig 69) **St Mary, Cleobury Mortimer** *Late Norman tower with broach-spire.*

Left: (Fig 70) **St John the Baptist, Ightfield** *Gargoyle and pinnacle on the top of the tower.*

(Fig 71) **St Peter, Worfield** *Decorated tower with recessed spire, the finest in Shropshire.*

Visiting Shropshire Churches

O VER 200 churches in Shropshire date back wholly, or in part, to medieval times, and it has not been easy to make a representative selection to tempt the readers of this book to venture exploring. People who visit churches usually want to see those in attractive surroundings; urban churches from Shrewsbury, Ludlow and Whitchurch are included, but the great majority of those illustrated here are village churches; and some are isolated and a little difficult to find. I have found that often the remotest and least-visited church can be the most rewarding; and in the pages that follow I often draw attention to those hidden treasures which await discovery. Although most of those chosen are of medieval origin, I have included a handful of post-Reformation churches down to the end of the nineteenth century.

It was difficult to know how to order the churches; an alphabetical list would have been arbitrary and without meaning; and there was no obvious geographical grouping. I finally opted for listing them in approximate order of building, beginning with those churches containing Saxon work, and ending with the nineteenth century. Of course, the order is very questionable, because most churches contain work from several centuries; in general, I have arranged them in chronological order determined by the building of the nave, because this gives more than anything else, the overall character of the building. The map shows the approximate location of all the churches illustrated; details of access are included at the end of the description of each church. The table may be found useful as a summary of the dates of the various architectural styles.

Map showing approximate location of the churches illustrated.

Date	Style	Representative Churches
Before 1066	Saxon	Barrow
1066-1100	Early Norman	Shrewsbury Holy Cross
1100-1150	Norman	Heath
		Morville
1160-1200	Late Norman	Linley
	Transitional	High Ercall
1200-1300	Early English	Cleobury Mortimer
		Acton Burnell
1300-1350	Decorated	Chelmarsh
1350-1550	Perpendicular	Edgmond, Ludlow
1550-1700	Elizabethan, Stuart	Langley, Minsterley
1700-1830	Georgian	Whitchurch,
		Shrewsbury St Chad
1830-1900	Victorian	Batchcott

St Andrew, Wroxeter

T HE church of St Andrew, Wroxeter, is more anciently steeped in history than any other in Shropshire. This of course derives from its proximity to the Roman fort of Viroconium, and masonry from there was plundered in the construction of the church about 1300 years ago. Cranage substantially deduced the complex building history of the church at the end of the nineteenth century, and nearly a hundred years later his conclusions have been largely substantiated by recent archaeological excavations. Detailed information is available in the church in the booklet published by the Redundant Churches Fund and in a reprint of a paper by Cameron Moffett from the Transactions of the Shropshire Archaeological and Historical Society.

The church now consists of chancel, nave and west tower, with a small vestry to the south-west of the chancel; previously there existed a south aisle, separated from the nave by an arcade. The history is best understood by walking round the exterior of the church, beginning with the north side (Fig.72; *see also* Fig.1, p8). The earliest part of the building is the eastern two-thirds of the north wall of the nave. This is built of Roman masonry, and dates from the seventh or eighth centuries. There is evidence of a small blocked square window high up in the wall; to the east

St Andrew, Wroxeter
(Fig 72) *View from the north.*

(Fig 73) *Part of a Saxon cross inserted in the south wall.*

Right: (Fig 77) *The font, thought to be the base of a Roman column.*

of this is a triple lancet window, which is a thirteenth-century insertion, and to the west of it is a later Perpendicular window. A string-course can be seen at the top of the wall, terminating to the west of the Perpendicular window, and just beyond this the boundary between the Saxon work and the rest of the nave can be discerned; there is a hint of Saxon long-and-short work at this margin.

In the twelfth century, the chancel was added; round-headed windows and a priest's door in the south wall remain. In the thirteenth century, three-light lancet windows were inserted in the north walls of the chancel and nave, and the nave was extended from the Saxon work westwards towards the tower. (The most westerly two-light window in the north wall is a Victorian insertion.) Probably also early in the thirteenth century a south aisle was built. The base of the tower appears to date from the fifteenth century, while the upper storeys are late Perpendicular (sixteenth century). In 1763, the thirteenth-century south aisle was demolished, and the present narrow aisle and vestry were built. Part of the shaft of a ninth century Saxon cross was set into

(Fig 74) *View from the chancel showing the Transitional chancel arch.*

(Fig 75) *Capital with stiff-leaf carving.*

(Fig 76) *Monument to Lord Chief Justice Bromley and his wife.*

(Fig 78) *Thirteenth-century chest.*

the top of the south wall; the carving is intricate, and a dragon, foliage scrolls and interlace may be discerned (Fig.73).

Internally, the late Norman chancel is fine, and there are two remaining Norman windows in the north wall, and two in the south. There is also the blocked priest's doorway in the south wall. The chancel arch is Transitional, being pointed, (Fig.74) and the capitals have stiff-leaf (Fig.75) and trumpet carving. In the north wall of the chancel is a Decorated recess (fourteenth century) adorned with ball-flower and trefoil patterns. The sixteenth and seventeenth-century monuments in the chancel are very fine, especially the alabaster effigies of Lord Chief Justice Bromley (died 1555) and his wife (Fig.76). An unusual feature of the Bromley tomb is the figure of their daughter holding a flower, and a pheasant at the head of the judge (Gardner). In the nave are a set of Jacobean box-pews. At the west end, note the enormous font, which is probably the base of a Roman column (Fig.77), and an impressive thirteenth-century chest (Fig.78).

In Anglo-Saxon times the church was collegiate and had four priests. It was given to Haughmond Abbey in the twelfth century, but the college was retained until 1347 when the abbey appointed a vicar. St Andrew's continued as a parish church until 1980 when it was declared superfluous for pastoral purposes, and since 1987 it has been in the care of the Redundant Churches Fund.

Access: Wroxeter is about six miles east of Shrewsbury. Proceed along the A5 and one mile past Attingham Park turn right (B4380). Take the second lane on the right off this road, passing the Roman ruins on the left. St Andrew's is a few hundred yards further on, on the left.

St Giles, Barrow

SITUATED on a lonely, windswept hillside, with just a farm for company, and little evidence of other habitation, St Giles' survival for perhaps 1200 years seems little short of miraculous. It would be difficult to say that the church is beautiful, but it impresses because of its very great antiquity, its plainness and simplicity, and perhaps above all because it is still a place of Christian worship.

The church consists of chancel, nave, and tower, and the building was in that order. The chancel is by far the oldest, and has been dated possibly to the eighth century, making

(Fig 80) **St Giles, Barrow** *Saxon chancel arch.*

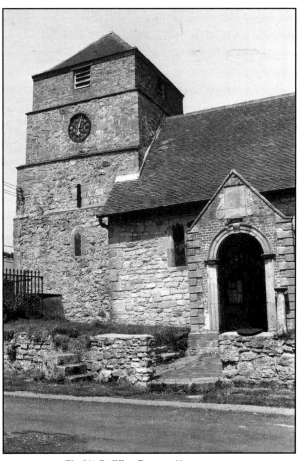
(Fig 81) **St Giles, Barrow** *Norman tower.*

(Fig 79) **St Giles, Barrow** *Saxon window, splayed externally as well as internally.*

it one of the most ancient churches in the country. It was subordinate to Wenlock Priory which had been founded in the late seventh century. Externally, on the north wall of the chancel, are the remains of a strip pilaster, and to the east of this on the same wall is a doubly splayed Saxon window (Fig.79). Internally, the very plain chancel arch is also Saxon, with what Pevsner describes as 'the characteristic square hood mould' (Fig.80).

Next is the nave, probably constructed in the late eleventh century, with round-headed windows in the north and south walls, and a Norman south doorway. The tower arch at the west end of the nave was originally the west doorway of the church, and if one goes into the present ground floor of the tower, one sees above the doorway a very early Norman tympanum, with rows of simple geometrical patterns (Fig.31, p19). The tower came last, probably about 1100, and it is surmounted by later battlements and pyramid roof (Fig.81). The south porch was built of brick in 1705.

Access: From Much Wenlock, take the B4376 towards Broseley. Barrow church is on the right of this road, three quarters of a mile after the B4375 leaves to the left.

St Peter, Diddlebury

D IDDLEBURY is an attractive village in Corvedale, and St Peter's is one of the handful in the county of indisputable Saxon origins, though not mentioned in the Domesday Book (Fig.82). Just after the Norman conquest, the church was granted by Earl Roger to Shrewsbury Abbey.

The Saxon work consists of the north wall of the nave, and part of the base of the tower. Typical herring-bone masonry is seen internally, where it has been repointed and looks much less ancient than it is (Fig.2, p9). Externally, there is a blocked north doorway described by Pevsner as 'typically Saxon with big shapeless block-like imposts and a raised moulding, square in section, framing the doorway and its arch' (Fig.4, p9). High in the north wall is a Saxon window, splayed outside and inside (Fig.2). In the base of the west wall of the tower is a very large

(Fig 83) **St Peter, Diddlebury** *Doorway and arch in the west wall of the tower.*

partially blocked Norman arch set above a Transitional west doorway (Fig.83).

The chancel is twelfth century, with Norman windows in both north and south walls. The east window is Victorian Decorated, but genuine early Decorated windows may be seen in the north and south walls of the chancel; in the north window may be seen some medieval glass representing the Crucifixion. Also in the chancel are two Decorated recesses with ball-flower ornament, that on the north side being an Easter sepulchre.

The tower arch is Transitional, and the arcade separating the nave from the south aisle is Early English. The south wall itself is nineteenth century.

Access: From Craven Arms, proceed along the B4368 towards Much Wenlock. Diddlebury is five miles from Craven Arms, the church being about 600 yards along a side road to the right.

(Fig 82) **St Peter, Diddlebury**

(Fig 84) **St Peter, Stanton Lacy**

These may be seen on the north and west walls of the nave and the west wall of the north transept, and have been dated to the mid-eleventh century. Most striking is the blocked Saxon doorway in the north wall of the nave; above the arch is a Saxon cross surmounted by a stone from which rises the pilaster strip above.

In the late thirteenth century, the chancel was rebuilt, and four windows in the north and south walls, though renewed, show the transition between Early English and Decorated tracery. Early in the next century came the south transept, the central tower, and the south aisle, separated from the nave by a Decorated arcade of two bays supported by an octagonal pier (Fig.85).

An excellent guide to the church by Peter Klein is available.

Access: From Ludlow, proceed north along A49 and after two miles turn right into B4365. One and a quarter miles further on, a lane on the right leads to Stanton Lacy; the church is on the left, immediately after crossing the river Corve.

St Peter, Stanton Lacy

The north and west walls of the nave and the west wall of the north transept are the finest Saxon work in Shropshire, and are clear evidence of a substantial pre-Conquest church here. This perhaps is not surprising when it is recalled that, as revealed by the number of its plough-teams and its population, the area was the richest and most productive land in Shropshire (Klein). At the Conquest, Stanton was held by a Saxon freeman Siward, but 20 years later by the time of the Domesday survey it was in the possession of Roger de Lacy, who also held Ewyas Lacy (now called Longtown) in Herefordshire. (Lacy is from Lassy in Normandy.) In 1103 the advowson was given to Llanthony Priory in the next valley to Ewyas Lacy.

The greatest interest of the church (Fig.84) is the external appearances of the Saxon walls which are ornamented by vertical strips (or pilasters Fig.3, p9).

Holy Cross, Shrewsbury
(Shrewsbury Abbey)

THE WEST front and tower of Shrewsbury Abbey (Fig.86) constitute one of the finest urban views in the county, familiar to all Shropshire folk. The existing parish church of the Holy Cross began as the Benedictine Abbey of St Peter and St Paul, which was founded by Earl Roger in 1083 on the site of a former wooden Anglo-Saxon church; originally, it was a daughter house of Seez, Normandy. After the Dissolution in 1540, the eastern part of the church was taken down, and the nave continued as a parish church; the existing east end of Holy Cross dates from a Victorian rebuilding in 1887.

The base of the west tower is Norman, and the remains of the original Norman west doorway survive. Above this is a fine fourteenth-century window, basically Perpendicular, but surmounted by an ogee crocketed canopy typical of the Decorated period (Fig.23, p16). The window therefore dates from the transitional period between the Decorated and Perpendicular styles, *c.*1360-70. Also Perpendicular is the three-storeyed north porch, although the inner

(Fig 85) **St Peter, Stanton Lacy** *The crossing and part of the south arcade.*

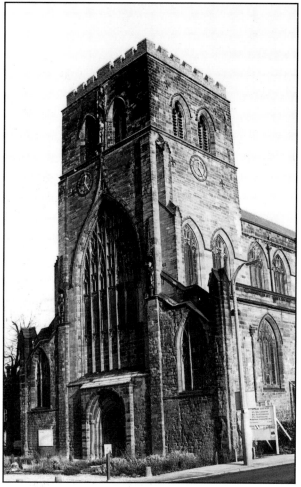

(Fig 86) **Holy Cross, Shrewsbury**

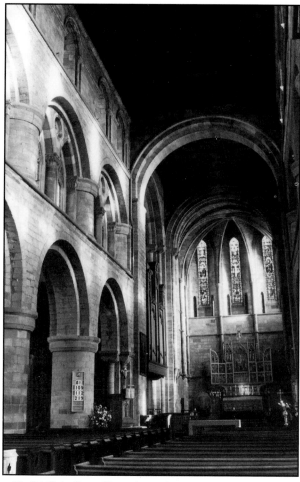

(Fig 87) **Holy Cross, Shrewsbury** *The Norman north arcade, and Victorian chancel.*

(Fig 88) **Holy Cross, Shrewsbury** *Arcade, triforium and clerestory.*

doorway of the porch is Norman.

On entering the church, one is immediately struck by the contrast between the three eastern bays of the nave, which are very early Norman (*c.*1090) and the two western bays, which are Perpendicular. The three Norman bays have big round piers supporting semicircular arches (Fig.87); above them is the triforium, originally Norman, but modified in the fourteenth century; and above this the clerestory which dates from the Victorian reconstruction (Fig.88). The arch from the north aisle into the transept is eleventh century, but beyond, the whole of the crossing and chancel date from 1887. At the western end of the nave, the Perpendicular arcades are surmounted by a clerestory but no triforium. The tower arch is also Perpendicular. The font is thought to be made from a Roman capital.

Access: On the east bank of the River Severn; from the town centre, walk down Wyle Cop, cross the river, and the Abbey is seen just to the left.

St Gregory, Morville

TODAY Morville is a small village west of Bridgnorth, but its importance in earlier times was much greater. It was the centre of an extensive Saxon parish, which included Bridgnorth and reached as far as Billingsley, Astley Abbots, and Cold Weston. It was a collegiate church staffed by eight canons. After the Conquest, Earl Roger gave it to Shrewsbury Abbey; in 1138 Morville became a Benedictine priory, a daughter cell of Shrewsbury, and so it remained until the Reformation.

The church is one of the few Norman buildings of which there is documentary evidence of the date of construction, for a statement in the Chronicle of Florence of Worcester says 'In 1118, Geoffrey de Clive, Bishop of Hereford consecrated a new church at Morville which had been built by the monks of Shrewsbury'; he goes on to relate that after the

(Fig 89) **St Gregory, Morville**

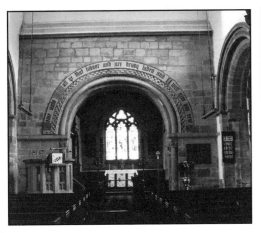

Left: (Fig 90) *Norman chancel arch and arcade.*

Middle: (Fig 91) *Norman font.*

Right: (Fig 92) *Twelfth-century ironwork on the south door.*

consecration, two women and five horses were struck by lightning and killed (Cranage).

St Gregory's is a spacious and dignified Norman church now set in parkland next to Morville Hall (Fig.89). The church was built in phases during the twelfth century, beginning with the nave and chancel in 1118; this was followed by the tower, and lastly by the aisles. The chancel arch (Fig.90) is decorated with the 'billet' pattern – short raised rectangles repeated at regular intervals. The arcades are supported by square piers with shafts of the late twelfth century; the capitals have upright leaves. The font (Fig.91) is a Norman tub, carved with medallions and human faces. Note the excellent ironwork on the door, some of which is 800 years old (Fig.92). The clerestory was added in the nineteenth century.

At the Reformation the priory was disbanded and on its site an Elizabethan hall was built. This was refaced in the eighteenth century, and is now owned by the National Trust.

Access: Take the A458 westwards from Bridgnorth towards Much Wenlock. St Gregory's is on the left, just before the junction with the B4368.

Heath Chapel

HEATH is an ancient chapelry of the parish of Stoke St Milborough, and the chapel is the sole relic of the medieval village. As explained earlier (p10), the uplands around Brown Clee Hill were always marginal land, and as the climate worsened in the later Middle Ages the population declined and several villages withered away. So the chapel stands quite alone in a field (Fig.93), its modest and somewhat unprepossessing appearance belying the fact that it is possibly the most famous church in Shropshire.

The reason why it is so justly celebrated is because the building has been left virtually unaltered for 850

(Fig 93) **Heath Chapel**

Above: (Fig 94)
Heath Chapel
*Box-pews and
chancel arch.*

Right:(Fig 95)
Heath Chapel
Norman doorway.

frieze of incised arcading around the top. The pulpit and box-pews date from the seventeenth century. Medieval wall-paintings survive, and were apparently discovered only in 1911, having been previously hidden by plaster. At the time of writing, these paintings await conservation.

Access: Heath lies between Corvedale and Brown Clee Hill, and the chapel is not very easy to find. From Craven Arms, proceed along B4368 towards Much Wenlock. After six miles, turn right in Diddlebury village, and after a short distance you pass Diddlebury church on your right. The lane then winds for 1½ miles, crossing the Trow Brook; take the first turning right to Peaton, then turn left; after a further mile turn left again, and then immediately fork right. Heath is one mile from this point, the chapel being in a field on the left. The key is readily available at the farm 340 yards beyond the chapel.

All Saints, Claverley

The quality of the medieval wall-paintings uncovered in Claverley in 1902 places this church in the very front rank of Shropshire churches. Situated in a most attractive village, a visit to Claverley is a 'must' for all church-lovers.

Claverley is 'clover meadow' and was mentioned in the Domesday Book as 'Claverlege'. There was probably a Saxon church here, though it is not mentioned in Domesday. The manor was held by Earl Roger and the church was connected with the collegiate foundation which he endowed at Quatford; later it was transferred to Bridgnorth. The earliest part of the present church is the west wall and parts of the

(Fig 96) **All Saints, Claverley** *The north arcade with the wall-paintings above.*

years – the single change being a modification of the window in the north wall of the nave about 300 years ago. The church consists of just a nave and chancel, and was built *c*.1140. The windows are small, round-headed and deeply splayed. The chancel arch (Fig.94) is simple and plain, though the flanking shafts have capitals with scallops and volutes. The south doorway (Fig.95) shows much chevron decoration, now rather worn, and the door retains some twelfth-century wrought ironwork. The font is a Norman tub, with a

north wall of the nave; these are Norman, probably of the first half of the twelfth century; they are followed by the impressive north arcade of solid round piers supporting semicircular arches (Fig.96). A little later came the lower part of the tower. The south aisle was added in the mid-thirteenth century, and has octagonal piers, and capitals with heads, beasts and upright leaves. The west window of the nave shows intersecting tracery, indicating that it was inserted into the Norman wall *c*.1300. In the Decorated period

(Fig 97) **All Saints, Claverley**
The porch.

(Fig 98) *The font.*

splendid tomb of Sir Robert Broke, Speaker of the House of Commons, who died in 1558. He is seen with his two wives, the second of whom was born Dorothy Gatacre. On the east wall of the chapel are two large incised alabaster slabs commemorating Sir William Gatacre (1577) and his wife, and Francis Gatacre (1599) and his wife (Fig.37, p20)

But of course the greatest treasure of Claverley, which makes the church one of national importance, is the medieval wall-painting above the Norman north arcade (Figs.100 and 101). This has been dated to *c*.1200, and at first was thought to

(mid-fourteenth century) the chancel was rebuilt; the east window is a fine example of Decorated tracery. The clerestory, the south chapel, the fine porch (Fig.97) and the upper storeys of the tower (Fig.99) are Perpendicular. The roof of the nave is of low pitch, panelled and boarded, with extra decoration over the easternmost bay forming a 'ceilure' above the former rood 'heavily ornamented with square flowers and leaves' (A.R.Green, cited by Vallance; Fig.50, p24) The roof of the chancel is of the hammer-beam type, with arched braces and collar-beams.

There are two fonts: the earlier plain one may be Saxon or early Norman; the later is certainly Norman, showing arches carved above patterned columns (Fig.98). In the south chapel (The Gatacre chapel) is a

portray the Battle of Hastings – because of a supposed resemblance to the Bayeux tapestry. Expert opinion has now concluded that the series is a representation of the conflict between seven Christian virtues and seven pagan vices, depicted as a battle between equestrian knights. The paintings are lively and in a remarkably good state of preservation. Between the windows of the clerestory and in the spandrels of the arches may be seen other painting of a much later date – fifteenth century. Over the chancel arch may be seen part of a Doom (representing the Last Judgment), also probably of fifteenth-century origin.

Access: From Bridgnorth, take the A454 towards Wolverhampton for four miles, and then turn right for Claverley.

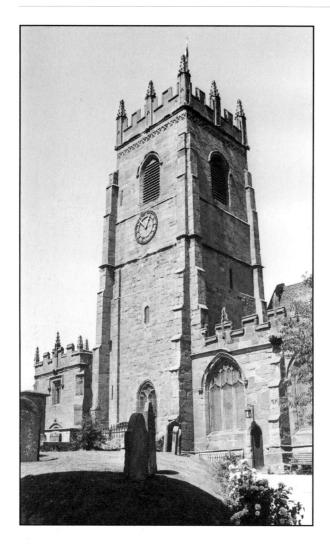

All Saints, Claverley Far left: (Fig 99) *The tower.*

Left, top and bottom: (Figs.100 & 101) *Details of the wall-paintings.*

(Fig 103) **St Mary, Stottesdon** *The Norman north arcade.*

St Mary, Stottesdon

STOTTESDON – the 'hill of the herd of horses' – is now a rather out-of-the-way village, but, like Morville, in Saxon times it was the centre of a far-flung parish. The church was given by Earl Roger to Shrewsbury Abbey and it has one remarkable survival from the eleventh century – the tympanum over the former west door. The other outstanding treasure of the church is the Norman font. The building history of St Mary's may be summarised as follows: early Norman, the base of the tower; late Norman, the arcades separating the aisle from the nave (only the north survives in its original form); Decorated (fourteenth century) the chancel and eastward exten-sion of the aisles;

(Fig 102) **St Mary, Stottesdon** *The finest Norman font in Shropshire.*

Perpendicular (fifteenth century) the upper part of the tower.

The tympanum (Fig.33, p19) is of course of outstanding interest because of its antiquity, but it would be difficult to describe it as beautiful. It is placed above the former west doorway; now it is inside the tower, behind the organ, in a rather obscure position. It was carved in the eleventh century, either late Saxon or early Norman, and must be earlier than the base of the tower. At the apex of the triangle is a grotesque bearded head, and on the lintel are carved some strange beasts in bizarre postures,

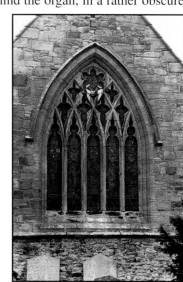

(Fig 104) **St Mary, Stottesdon** *Decorated east window of chancel.*

possibly representing a chase. The upper part of the tympanum is ornamented with upright and diagonal lines.

In contrast to the tympanum, there are no qualms about the beauty of the late Norman font (Fig.102), described by Pevsner as follows: 'The most sumptuous Norman font in Shropshire, probably of *c.*1160, and work of the Hereford School whose more famous carvings are at Shobdon, Kilpeck, etc. Bands of scrolls and leaves on foot and stem. On the bowl below a band of ribbed interlace a series of medallions with the lamb and cross, beasts, a frontal figure of a man with parallel ribbing to represent drapery, and leaf motifs.'

The arcade separating the north aisle from the nave is late twelfth century, with massive circular columns supporting round arches (Fig.103); the south arcade was rebuilt in 1867. The chancel is Decorated, and has a beautiful geometric east window like Kinlet and Chelmarsh (Fig.104). Curvilinear tracery may be seen in the east window of the south aisle. Note the fine sedilia (seats for the priests) in the south wall of the chancel.

Access: From Bridgnorth, take the B4363 south towards Cleobury Mortimer; after about six miles, turn right at Billingsley and this lane passes through Chorley village and then reaches Stottesdon. The church is not very easy to find: it is at the end of a narrow lane which leaves the centre of the village on the right.

St Leonard, Linley

THE little church stands alone, along a drive leading to Linley Hall. It consists of a Norman tower, nave and chancel, dating from the second half of the twelfth century, and has never been enlarged, though a good deal restored.

Externally, the tympana of both north and south doorways are worth noting. Above the blocked north doorway is carved a pagan fertility figure, a 'green man' or sheila-na-gig. Similar figures may be seen at Church Stretton, Holdgate and Tugford. The tympanum of the south doorway is carved with zigzags.

Internally the plain chancel arch is pointed (i.e. Transitional) and the tower arch round (Fig.105). The half-columns supporting the tower arch have capitals carved with scrolls and nail-heads (Fig.106). There are Norman windows in the north and south walls of the chancel; the lancet windows in the east wall are Victorian. The windows in the Norman nave are later insertions of the fourteenth or fifteenth century. The font is finely carved with cable ornament, foliage and grotesque heads (Fig.107).

Access: From Broseley, proceed south along B4373 towards Bridgnorth. After three miles a narrow drive forks to the left, signposted Linley church; St Leonard's is a short distance along on the left. The

Above: (Fig 105) **St Leonard, Linley** *Norman tower arch.*

Right: (Fig 106) **St Leonard, Linley** *North capital of tower arch.*

church is usually locked, but a notice informs visitors where the key may be obtained nearby.

(Fig 107) **St Leonard, Linley** *The font.*

St Michael, Onibury

ONIBURY lies in the valley of the Onny, downstream from Stokesay, and is graced by St Michael's church, a basically Norman building. It consists simply of chancel, nave and tower. The tower is squat and battlemented. The interior of the church is appealing: there is a plain round arch separating nave and chancel (Fig.108). The east windows of the chancel are Early English lancets. The nave roof has tie-beams and queen-posts (Fig.43 p22)

Below: (Fig 108) **St Michael, Onibury** *Norman chancel arch.*

Right: (Fig 109) **St Michael, Onibury** *Medieval pulpit.*

and there is a west gallery dating from a restoration in 1902. Notable also is the oldest pulpit in any Shropshire church – Perpendicular with some Jacobean additions (Fig.109).

Access: From Ludlow, proceed north along A49 for about five miles; the turning to the right leads across the railway line to the village, with St Michael's on the left.

St Michael, Upton Cressett

A VISIT to this remote church is a memorable experience: firstly, there is the difficulty in finding it, and then the joy of discovering such a treasure in this isolated spot (Fig.110). For St Michael's stands, with its neighbour the Elizabethan hall, at the end of a long lane; and it is a marvellously unspoilt Norman building with thirteenth-century additions.

(Fig 110) **St Michael, Upton Cressett**

The Upton family dates from Saxon times, and was joined in marriage to the Cressetts in the fourteenth century. The church dates from the second half of the twelfth century, and the Norman arches are exceeded in quality in Shropshire only by those of Edstaston. The most remarkable is the chancel arch, which has four orders of zigzag and other mouldings (Fig.111); originally it was surmounted by a hood-mould, a fragment of which can still be seen at the south end of the arch. The south doorway in the nave is also a fine Norman arch, somewhat hidden by the later porch. The font is Norman, with cable moulding at top and bottom, and carved arches around the bowl (Fig.112). There are Norman round-headed windows in the west and south walls of the nave, and the north wall of the chancel. The east window in the chancel is a very unusual single lancet, possibly inserted in the thirteenth century. Also in the thirteenth century two further additions were made to the church: a north

aisle was built (later demolished) and the arcade of this can be seen bonded in the north wall of the nave; and a chapel was built to the south of the chancel. This is joined to the chancel by an Early English arch. In the west wall of the chapel, a medieval wall-painting was uncovered in 1968, similar in style to those of Claverley.

Top: (Fig 111) **St Michael, Upton Cressett** *Norman chancel arch.* and below, (Fig 112) *The font.*

St Michael's was closed for worship in 1959, and since 1972 has been in the care of the Redundant Churches Fund.

Access: An adventure! From Bridgnorth, take the A458 road towards Much Wenlock. After three miles, the lane to Upton Cressett is sign-posted to the left.

Follow this lane to the very end, over the Mor brook and past the township of Meadowley. The lane becomes ever narrower, and the church is rather hidden behind trees on the right side, just before the hall.

St John the Baptist, Hope Bagot

THIS is a little-known gem on the south slopes of Titterstone Clee Hill (Fig.113). A small Norman church, consisting only of nave, chancel and tower, it appeals because of its utter simplicity, some might say naïvety. The chancel arch (Fig.114) is lovely; there is hatching ornamentation on the outer order, on the top of the capitals and on the string-course continuing from the abaci to the walls of the nave and chancel. The south doorway is rather similar. There is a fine deeply-splayed Norman window in the north wall of the chancel (Fig.11, p11), and another in the north wall of the nave. In the south wall of the chancel are two thirteenth-century windows; under the one further east is a sedile with a stone arm at the left and a deeply cut piscina to the right. In the south wall of the nave is a fourteenth-century window. The west gallery dates from 1726. There is a plain Norman font.

'Hope' probably means 'small enclosed valley'; Bagot comes from Robert Bagard who held the manor

(Fig 113) **St John the Baptist, Hope Bagot**

(Fig 114) **St John the Baptist, Hope Bagot** *Norman chancel arch.*

in 1242, Bagard being a French family name.

Access: From Ludlow, take the A4117 eastward towards Kidderminster, and after 5½ miles turn right at Cleehill into B4274 towards Burford. After just over a mile, turn right, and then right again, for Hope Bagot. The church is on the left.

(Fig 115) **St Mary, Edstaston** *South chancel doorway.*

St Mary, Edstaston

S T MARY'S deserves to be better known for it has the finest Norman doorways in Shropshire, remarkable in a building which was but a subsidiary chapel in the parish of Wem until 1852. Of the three doorways, the priest's in the south wall of the chancel is the simplest (Fig.115), with carving of the zigzag and dog-tooth patterns. The north door-way (Fig.116) 'shows a carved head in the middle of the dripstone; below this is a plain hollow, and then a very beautiful band for carving, displaying dragons, heads, and the figure of a woman. The inner order is a zigzag enclosing a round: it rests on shafts with excellent foliated capitals. There is excellent iron-work on the door. Still finer is the main south doorway, the richest in the county (Figs.117 and 118). The dripstone has a double dog-tooth moulding: the three carved heads seem to be coeval. The next three orders dis-play varieties of the zigzag: the innermost order has the embat-tled moulding. The abaci of the capitals are almost Early

(Fig 116) *North doorway.*

(Fig 117) *Norman south doorway, the finest in Shropshire.*

English in their undercutting. The foliage is not quite of the 'stiff-leaf' form but is a near approximation to it. One of the eastern capitals has some quaint animal carving, and one has a head in the middle of the foliage.' (Cranage). Again there is some good ironwork on the door.

Note also the Norman corbel-table of trefoiled

(Fig 118) *Details of arch over south doorway.*

(Fig 119) *Norman window, with nook-shafts and arch, and corbel-table above.*

(Fig 120) *Decorated east window.*

arches which runs externally beneath the eaves; and the large Norman window with a decorated arch above it in the north wall of the nave (Fig.119). The chancel was rebuilt in the fourteenth century, and the fine east window of five lights shows Decorated tracery of the 'geometric' type, with a spheric triangle in the head (Fig.120). Other windows in the nave and chancel are Perpendicular insertions. The roof of the nave has tie-beams with king-posts and two tiers of wind-braces.

Access: From Wem, proceed north along the Whitchurch road (B5475); after two miles, the turning to Edstaston is on the left, and St Mary's is 300 yards along this lane on the right.

St James, Shipton

SHIPTON (meaning 'sheep farm') and its church are mentioned in the Domesday Book, and the nave and lower part of the tower do indeed date from the late twelfth century. But St James is remarkable nowadays for its Elizabethan chancel, and the church is nicely situated next to the fine Elizabethan hall. Externally, the nave and tower (Fig.122), which is weather-boarded with a pyramidal roof, are buff-coated and are not, perhaps, specially attractive; internally, it is quite a different matter.

The interior is simple and serene, the Norman nave contrasting well with the Elizabethan chancel. The tower arch is Transitional (*c.*1200) and pointed; the chancel arch is Norman and round (Fig.121). On either side of the latter are large squints, which may or may not be of the twelfth century.

The chancel is of great interest to architectural historians because of the great rarity of Elizabethan church building. A notice records that:

'THIS CHANCEL WAS REEDIFIED AND BUILDED OF NEWE FROM THE FOUNDACION, AND GLASED AT THE CHARGES OF JOHN LUTWICH, YOUNGEST SONNE OF RICHARD LUTWICH OF LUTWICHE; IN THE XXXI YEARE OF THE GRACIOUS REIGNE OF QUEENE ELIZABETH. 1589'.

The east window is constructed in the Decorated style of 250 years earlier, and the lower part of the

(Fig 121) **St James, Shipton** *View from chancel into nave, showing Norman chancel arch and Transitional tower arch.*

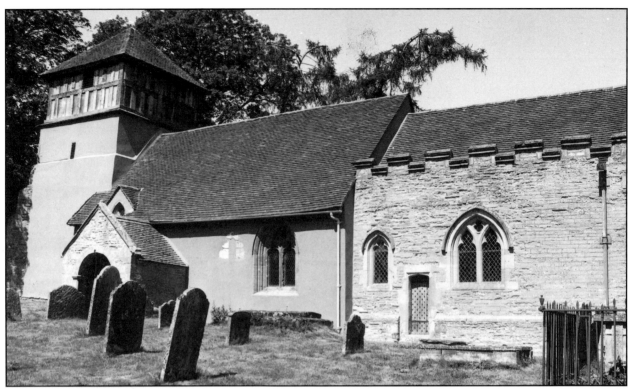

(Fig 122) **St James, Shipton** *Norman nave and tower, and Elizabethan chancel.*

(Fig 123) **St Catherine, Tugford**

window contains some original stained glass. Also original are the iron stanchions of the windows. The roof is of the trussed-rafter type.

Access: From Much Wenlock, proceed south-west along B4378 towards Craven Arms. Shipton is about seven miles along this road, the church of St James being on the right.

St Catherine, Tugford

TUGFORD is prettily situated in Corvedale, at the foot of Brown Clee Hill, with St Catherine's Church (Fig.123) set a little way back from the lane, with access across a small meadow.

The nave dates from the mid-twelfth century, with

(Fig 124) **St Catherine, Tugford** *Norman south doorway.*

the south doorway (Fig.124) showing one order of shafts on each side. The arch above has lozenge decoration. High up on either side of the doorway are two small sheila-na-gigs (fertility symbols). There is a Norman window in the north wall of the nave. The chancel is later, Early English, with windows mainly of the early Decorated type presumably inserted later here and in the nave. The tower is also Early English, with later battlements. There is a west gallery, which is said to have been partly made from components of the former screen.

Access: From Craven Arms, take the B4368 towards Bridgnorth; at Beambridge, half a mile after Munslow, turn right; at the T-junction turn left, then right, and this lane leads to Tugford

(Fig 125) **St Mary, Shawbury** *Norman font and north arcade.*

St Mary, Shawbury

SHAWBURY is a good example of a beautiful parish church with representation of every medieval building style from the Norman era onwards. Perhaps it would make for clarity if we proceeded chronologically.

There was a church here in Saxon times, mentioned in the Domesday Book (the manor was held by Gerard from the ubiquitous Earl Roger), but nothing remains of this building. The arcades in the nave are twelfth-century Norman (Fig.125), and they are, as Pevsner says, complete and beautifully proportioned. Notice how the westernmost arcade has been truncated by the later building of the tower. The piers are circular, and their capitals are decorated with scallops (Fig.7, p11).

Both the north and south doorways are Norman, as is the font (Fig.126). Moving into the thirteenth century (Early English) there is the pointed arch to the chancel, and two blocked lancet windows in the chancel. The Decorated period (fourteenth century) is represented by the east window for the south aisle. To the Perpendicular age (fif-

(Fig 126) **St Mary, Shawbury** *The font.*

(Fig 127) **St John the Baptist, Kinlet** *View from the south.*

teenth and sixteenth centuries) belong the north aisle, north chapel and the tower (Fig.66, p28). In the seventeenth century the north porch was built. There is a Jacobean pulpit and an eighteenth century brass chandelier.

Access: Take the A49 north from Shrewsbury and just after the ghastly retail park at Harlescott, turn right into the A53; Shawbury is just over four miles along this road, St Mary's being just a little off the main road on the right.

St John the Baptist, Kinlet

KINLET is the finest imparked church in Shropshire (Fig.127), standing alone near to Kinlet Hall. This is the result of the creation of Kinlet Park in the early eighteenth century, when the village was extinguished and the road diverted (Rowley). The church is not very easy to find, but it is so good that it is well worth making the effort to do so.

At the time of the Norman Conquest the manor was held by Queen Edith, wife of Edward the Confessor, and the name 'Kinlet' appears to mean 'royal share or portion'. The church dates back to Norman times, and here are very fine semicircular Norman arcades separating the nave from the aisles, the north being a little earlier than the south (Fig.6, p10, and Fig.128). The tower arch is Early English (Fig.6), with capitals showing stiff-leaf decoration and heads. The chancel, north and south transepts were built 100 years later in

(Fig 128) *Norman north arcade and Decorated chancel arch.*

the Decorated period. The chancel arch (Fig.128) is very fine, with three orders, and the east window to the chancel shows excellent Decorated tracery, similar to those at Stottesdon and Chelmarsh (Fig.130; cf. Fig.104, p40). In the Perpendicular period, a half-timbered clerestory combined with a trussed-rafter and collar-beam roof was added to the nave.

But in addition to all this, Kinlet church is notable for its fine array of monuments. In the east window of the south transept is an alabaster figure of the Trinity, and in the wall opposite, also in alabaster, the effigy of a lady, probably Isobel, daughter of Sir John Cornwall (*c.*1420); by her side is an infant wrapped in swaddling clothes, possibly indicating that the mother died in childbirth (Gardner). In the chancel are two

(Fig 129) *Monument to Sir George Blount and his wife (1584).*

Right: (Fig 130) *Decorated east window.*

Far right, top: (Fig 131) *Monument to Sir Humphrey Blount and his wife (1477).*

Far right, bottom: (Fig 132) *Monument to Sir John Blount and his wife (1531).*

further tomb-chests with alabaster effigies commemorating Sir Humphrey Blount (died 1477; Fig.131) and Sir John Blount (died 1531, Fig.132) and their respective wives; the former knight is Yorkist, but the latter wears the SS collar denoting allegiance to the House of Lancaster, who had by this time gained the crown in the person of Henry VII. But dwarfing all these, both literally and metaphorically, is the monument to Sir George Blount and his wife in the north transept (Fig.129) – one of the finest Elizabethan monuments in the country. It is fascinating to observe the evolution in styles of the three Blount monuments: the first (1477) medieval; the second (1531) renaissance; the third (1584) Elizabethan.

Access: Kinlet is on the B4363 from Bridgnorth to Cleobury Mortimer, situated about 4½ miles from the latter. The entrance to the park is immediately opposite the Eagle and Serpent inn. Go along the drive for about three quarters of a mile, and after crossing a cattle-grid turn left at the end of the next field towards a green gate, just beyond which is a footbridge. Walk through the gate and under the bridge into the churchyard. The church is mostly locked, but usually a notice informs visitors where the key may be obtained.

(Fig 133) **St Eata, Atcham**

St Eata, Atcham

S T EATA'S has a lovely situation on the east bank of the Severn (Fig.133), close to the old Georgian bridge which used to carry the A5 over the river. When I went there in May, nesting house-martins from the bridge were skimming over a pair of swans with their young on the river, and anglers were absorbing the beauty of the scene.

Atcham (or Attingham) means the 'ham' (homestead) of Eata's people, and the dedication of the church to St Eata is said to be unique. Eata was a friend of St Cuthbert, and was in turn abbot of Old Melrose and of Lindisfarne (664). There was a church here in Saxon times, and it is mentioned in the Domesday Book (1087). In 1075, the Anglo-Norman historian Ordericus Vitalis was baptised here; he lived at the abbey of St Evroul in Normandy, and wrote the history of Normandy and England (Historia Ecclesiastica) between 1123 and 1141.

Nothing remains of the Saxon church, the earliest part of the present building being the Norman window in the north wall of the nave. Roman stones were, however, re-used in the construction of the lower parts of the thirteenth-century tower, the upper part of the tower being Perpendicular (Fig.63, p28).

The fine west doorway of the tower has five orders of shafts, but has been much renewed.

The chancel is Early English (thirteenth century), with three lancet windows under one arch in the east window, and Y-tracery in the north and south windows; apart from the small Norman window, the other nave windows are Perpendicular insertions. Good sixteenth-century stained glass was brought from Bacton in Herefordshire in 1811. The roofs show tie-beams in the chancel, and arched braces and collar-beams in the nave (Fig.45, p22). The half-timbered south porch is dated 1685.

Access: Atcham is on the A5, 3½ miles southeast from Shrewsbury; the church is opposite the entrance to Attingham Park (National Trust).

St Michael, Lydbury North

T HE village is so called to distinguish it from Ledbury in Herefordshire, and it is mentioned as belonging to the Bishop of Hereford in Domesday Book. The church is large and dignified, with a long nave and two transepts, the Plowden chapel to the north and the Walcot chapel to the south. Both the nave and chancel are Norman, the former being earlier (the Norman windows being larger in the chancel than in the nave) and the massively buttressed tower is thirteenth century (Fig.134). The arch to the Plowden chapel is Norman, but the chapel itself was built in the fourteenth century. The Walcot chapel is seventeenth century, and the arch to it dates only from the restoration of 1901.

But perhaps what impresses most in St Michael's is

Top: (Fig 134) **St Michael, Lydbury North** *Early English tower with later battlements.*

Bottom: (Fig 135) **St Michael, Lydbury North** *Interior looking east.*

the quality of the wood-work. The interior (Fig. 135) is domi-nated by the much restored m e d i e v a l screen, and above it is an e x t e n s i v e t y m p a n u m dated 1615, on which is painted the Creed and C o m m a n d - ments. Before the Refor-mation, of course, there would have been the rood above the screen, and the staircase to the former rood-loft can be seen from the Plowden chapel. The nave roof is fine, with collar-beams and arched braces, and one pair of wind-braces with quatrefoil patterns. Finally, there is a Jacobean pulpit, and an excellent set of Jacobean box-pews.

Access: Lydbury North is on B4385, three miles south-east of Bishop's Castle.

Holy Trinity, Much Wenlock

M UCH Wenlock is a most attractive small Shropshire town, dominated by the ruins of the Priory, the most ancient Christian foundation in the county (*c*.680). As we have seen, it was originally a convent for monks and nuns, the king's daughter, Mildburge, being the first abbess. It is thought that Holy Trinity church was originally built for worship by the nuns, and St Mildburge was originally buried in the Lady Chapel of this church; her remains were transferred to the Priory church in 1101. Visitors to the famous Priory should not, however, overlook the ancient parish church of the Holy Trinity (Fig.136), for there is much to admire there.

The nave of the present church dates back to the mid-twelfth century, the most impressive Norman

(Fig 136) **Holy Trinity, Much Wenlock**

structure being the wide chancel arch (Fig.137) separating the nave from the chancel. Remains of a blocked-up Norman window may be seen high up in the south wall of the chancel. The west tower is later Norman (Transitional).

(Fig 137) **Holy Trinity, Much Wenlock** *Norman chancel arch and Early English south arcade.*

(Fig 138) **Holy Trinity, Much Wenlock** *Sedilia in south wall of the chancel.*

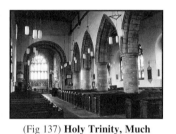

In the thirteenth century, the church was extended by the addition of a south aisle; it is separated from the nave by an arcade of still substantial piers, though the arches are pointed. Also in the Early English period was added the fine two-storey porch.

In the fourteenth century, the chancel was extended eastwards, the vaulted sedilia (Fig.138) in the south wall of the chancel dating from this time. The east window is early Perpendicular, though still with an ogee-shaped gable above it externally recalling the Decorated style. The pulpit is Jacobean.

Access: In the centre of the small town, nearly opposite the east end of the High Street.

St Bartholomew, Moreton Corbet

ST Bartholomew's church (Fig.139) and the ruins of the castle next door make an enchanting picture which somewhat belies their often turbulent history. The Corbets were one of the families of great Marcher lords who dominated Shropshire for centuries. The founder of the family, Roger Fitz Corbet, came from Caux in Normandy, and he was given extensive lands in the west of Shropshire at the end of the eleventh century. In return for safeguarding their territory from Welsh incursions, the Marcher lords were given powers from the twelfth century onwards to run their lands almost as independent states, collecting dues paid to Welsh lords and feudal incomes from their English manors. The system lasted until the statute incorporating Wales and England was enacted in the reign of Henry VIII (1536).

The Norman church at Moreton was founded about 1140 as a chapel attached to Shawbury, and the manor was held by Richard Corbet *c.*1200. The long association of the Corbet family with this church lasted into the twentieth century, for the stained glass in the east window of the chancel is in memory of Vincent Corbet who died aged 13 in 1904. Some parts of the north wall of the Norman church remain (there is a Norman window in the north wall of the chancel), but the greater part of the church dates from the fourteenth century. The south aisle was added in 1330-1340 by the Corbets, probably as a private chapel; at

(Fig 139) **St Bartholomew, Moreton Corbet**

(Fig 140) **St Bartholomew, Moreton Corbet** *Monument to Sir Robert Corbet and his wife (1513).*

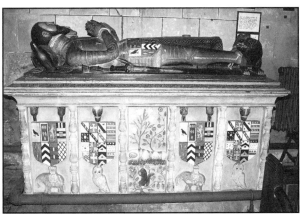

(Fig 141) **St Bartholomew, Moreton Corbet** *Monument to Sir Richard Corbet and his wife (1567).*

the west end is a most unusual triangular window – a very similar window of about the same date exists in Alberbury, which was another of the Corbet family's possessions. There are some striking sixteenth-century tombs in this aisle – of Sir Robert Corbet and his wife (d.1513; Fig.140) and Sir Richard and his wife (d.1567; Fig.141). In 1778 the squire's pew was built as an off-shoot of the south aisle. The lower part of the tower is Perpendicular, built *c.*1530, the upper stages being rebuilt in 1769.

Access: From Shrewsbury, take the A49 north for about nine miles; the turning to Moreton Corbet is on the right.

St Mary the Virgin, Shrewsbury

THAT the finest parish church in Shrewsbury should no longer be used for regular worship must strike the visitor as sad, perverse, astonishing. Yet it is so, and St Mary's is now in the care of the excellent Redundant Churches Fund. In the 1920s it was nearly raised to cathedral status, when its future would have been assured; but this proposal failed, and sixty years later the Church of England decided that it had no further use for the building for the foreseeable future. I hope that one day it will be restored for its original purpose of witness and worship, perhaps as an ecumenical centre; meanwhile the fabric is being very well maintained.

St Mary's dominates Shrewsbury (Fig.142), being built at its highest point, and the spire, attaining a height of 222 feet, is one of the tallest in the country. The church was originally a Saxon foundation, and later became a collegiate church consisting of a Dean, seven Prebendaries and a parish priest. The foundations of the preceding Saxon church were found under the present nave during excavations in the nineteenth century. This church must have been demolished around 1140 when a cruciform Norman church was built. This consisted of a nave and chancel, with crossing supporting a central tower, and north and south transepts. The arches separating the north chapels of St Nicholas and St Catherine from the north transept date from this time. Later in the twelfth century (c.1170), the lower stages of the west tower were built, with a pointed (Transitional) tower arch separating the tower from the west end of the nave.

At the very end of the twelfth century, when Norman (Transitional) architecture was giving way to Early English, the church was enlarged, and began to take on its present aspect. Aisles were constructed on either side of the nave, separated from the nave by the arcades (Fig.143). Note that these are still semicircular (Gothic has not yet quite taken over), yet the piers are certainly not the solid round ones typical of earlier Norman building (cf. Holy Cross, Shrewsbury) but instead are slim, finely subdivided, and crowned by capitals of stiff-leaf foliage (Fig.14, p13) typical of the Early English style of the thirteenth century.

The pointed chancel arch is taller than the arcades and above it two two-light round-headed windows were inserted in 1894 (Fig.49, p23) The other arches from the crossing into the transepts and chancel are of similar style. Externally, the south porch was also built c.1200, and shows a round-arched doorway with three orders of shafts and a tall arch with zigzag and other motifs.

In the mid-fourteenth century the south or Trinity chapel was built and at about the same time the windows in the north chapel, partly Decorated and partly Perpendicular, were inserted. In the fifteenth century, a clerestory was built above the nave, and the fine nave roof was constructed (Fig.49). This is a

(Fig 142) **St Mary, Shrewsbury**

panelled roof of low pitch, richly adorned with delicately carved bosses at the intersections and cusped quatrefoils in the panels. The top stage of the western tower was added, surmounted by the spire. Also in the Perpendicular era the south aisle received its three fine windows.

St Mary's has one of the finest collection of stained glass in the country, mostly brought from elsewhere. The great east window of the chancel dates only from the Victorian restoration of 1858, but it contains the Jesse window (Fig.144) comprising English glass of the fourteenth century. It is believed that this glass was originally given to the Franciscan church in Shrewsbury, being later transferred to old St Chad's, and then in 1792 after the collapse of that church to St Mary's. It is known as the Jesse window because it represents the Tree of Jesse tracing the genealogy of

(Fig 144) **St Mary, Shrewsbury** *The Jesse window.*

(Fig 143) **St Mary, Shrewsbury** *Early thirteenth-century north arcade.*

Jesus back to David and David's father Jesse. The figure of Jesse is seen lying horizontally in a deep sleep on a mattress across the three centre lights; from him arises a vine which connects above with the figures of the kings and prophets of Israel, and the figures of Mary and Joseph with the infant Jesus, St Matthew and St Luke; above this are scenes depicting the Nativity, Baptism and Crucifixion.

Medieval German glass is seen in the north windows of the chancel, and in the window of the aisles. The best Victorian glass is in the east windows of the Trinity or south chapel.

Access: St Mary's is in the centre of Shrewsbury, at its highest point.

St Michael, High Ercall

ERCALL is said to be an old Welsh name for the district (Ekwall). High Ercall and Child's Ercall in the Domesday Book were Archelou and Arcalun respectively; in the thirteenth century, they were called Magna and Parva Ercalwe.

St Michael's (Fig.145) is attractively situated next to the Jacobean hall, and is basically a church of the end of the twelfth century (i.e. the Transitional period in which circular Norman piers co-exist with pointed Gothic arches) although there has been controversy concerning the extent of the rebuilding which took place after the Civil War. The arcades (Fig.146) are very fine, with capitals decorated with scrolls and leaves; on the third north pier are two human heads and two rams' heads. Find also the very early Norman tympanum which has been re-set in the north wall of the nave (Fig.34, p19). As noted previously, this represents the Tree of Life, and has been linked by Gethyn-Jones to a school of sculpture based at Dymock, Gloucestershire, and dated to around 1110-15. The north chapel and chancel are Decorated (fourteenth century), possibly paid for by the knight whose effigy lies between the two (Salter). The east window of the chancel has reticulated tracery of the

(Fig 145) **St Michael, High Ercall**

(Fig 146) **St Michael, High Ercall** *Transitional arcade and tower arch.*

Decorated period, and other windows are Perpendicular in style. The tower also is Perpendicular.

The fine double hammer-beam roof was certainly constructed in the 1650s after the Civil War.

Access: Take the A49 north from Shrewsbury and at the roundabout 1½ miles from the centre, turn right into B5062, and proceed for about seven miles along this road, passing Haughmond Abbey on the left. On approaching High Ercall, St Michael's is along a short lane on the right.

Aston Eyre

VISIT this church of no known dedication to see just one object: the magnificent tympanum (Fig.35, p19) over the south door, recently restored by English Heritage. Dean Cranage describes it as follows:

'It is a representation of our Lord's triumphal entry into Jerusalem. His left hand holds a palm branch and two fingers of the right hand are uplifted: the nimbus is in the form of a cross. An ass and its foal are represented, the former being ridden. In front a man with a beard throws a branch in the way, and behind, a beardless figure holds a garment. The carving is of course rude, but it is in splendid preservation and a very interesting specimen of the art of the period.'

The tympanum is the work of the Herefordshire School of sculpture and has been dated to around 1150, not long after the nave was built (probably by Robert Fitz Aer). The chancel is somewhat later, witness the chancel arch (Fig.12, p12) which is pointed and therefore Transitional in style, probably after 1160.

Access: From Bridgnorth, proceed along the A458 towards Much Wenlock, turning left after 3½ miles at Morville into the B4368. Aston Eyre is a small village just one mile from Morville, and the church is on the right.

St Edith, Eaton-Under-Haywood

This little-known church is a real treasure, situated in glorious countryside at the foot of Wenlock Edge (Fig.147). The building is dedicated to St Edith, who is said to have been the daughter of King Egbert of Wessex (reigned 802-39). He founded a Benedictine nunnery in the Forest of Arden which was moved to Polesworth in Warwickshire and dedicated to St Edith.

The nave and tower of the church are Norman, the chancel Early English. The tower is unusually sited at the south-east corner of the nave, and the bell-openings are of two round-arched lights separated by a dividing shaft and under a larger rounded arch. The roof of the nave shows tie-beams, with collar-beams on arched braces. Between this and the lower roof of the chancel is a tympanum painted with arms. There is an excellent seventeenth-century pulpit with its original canopy.

(Fig 147) **St Edith, Eaton-under-Haywood**

In the Early English chancel are three plain lancet windows of equal height – a most unusual arrangement (Fig.15, p13). The excellent roof of the chancel is of low pitch, panelled and embossed (Fig.48, p23). In the north wall of the chancel is a fourteenth-century recess with ball-flower decoration, and containing a life-size oaken effigy.

Access: From Church Stretton, take the B4371 towards Much Wenlock. Just over a mile along this road, turn right at Hope Bowdler and pass through Ticklerton to Eaton-under-Haywood.

St Michael, Munslow

MUNSLOW is situated very attractively in Corvedale, and the church (Fig.148) presents a pleasing prospect, especially with its very fine wooden Perpendicular porch (Fig.149).

(Fig 148) **St Michael, Munslow**

(Fig 149) **St Michael, Munslow** *Timber-framed Perpendicular porch.*

The lower part of the tower, and the tower arch, are Norman, the chancel Early English, the windows in the north aisle Decorated, and the arcade of this aisle and the upper part of the tower Perpendicular – so all four major periods of medieval church architecture are represented. Perhaps the most beautiful feature is the Decorated tracery in the north aisle windows, with arches above the apices of other arches (Fig.19, p15). Some of these windows contain good medieval stained glass. Also notable are a nice Perpendicular font (Fig.30, p19), an ancient chest, and some medieval bench-ends. In the nave, two doors with a connecting staircase formerly gave access to the rood-loft, which was supported by a corbel with an angel bearing a shield.

Access: From Craven Arms, take B4368 towards Much Wenlock; Munslow is about seven miles along this road, and St Michael's is at the end of a short lane on the left.

Holy Trinity, Holdgate

THE name of the village is derived from Helgot, a Norman who held the manor at the time of the Domesday survey and who built a castle here. The church must have followed fairly soon afterwards, for it is certainly of twelfth-century origin.

It is sad to record that the building is showing some signs of dilapidation and urgent remedial work appears to be required. It is hoped that this will become possible, for the church has two superb Norman treasures – the font and the south doorway. These are described by Cranage as follows:

'The font (Fig.150) is richly carved and remarkable. The upper moulding is the cable. Below is some interlaced work, similar to that often seen on early crosses. The nail-head ornament is also used and some grotesque representations of serpents. The lower part of the bowl is carved with foliage of a late Norman type, and below is a short stem with an upright zigzag. The base has four curious heads, and rests on a square block, which is placed on a much larger round plinth.

(Fig 150) **Holy Trinity, Holdgate** *The Norman font.*

Right: (Fig 151) **Holy Trinity, Holdgate** *Norman south doorway.*

Below: (Fig 152) **Holy Trinity, Holdgate** *Interior looking west.*

'The doorway (Fig.151) is of the same rich character and is twice recessed. The hood-moulding has pellets on the eastern and diminutive zigzag on the western half. The next moulding is a large zigzag, which does not stand out very boldly, as a reference to the photograph will show. Next to this are rosettes, foliage, and other forms, and the inner moulding is a row of rather poor beak-heads. All the shafts have ornamental capitals. On the east side small volutes are the principal enrichments, combined with foliage on two out of the three. Two of the western capitals also have foliage, combined in one case with nail-heads; the outer capital is scalloped. The bases are slightly ornamented.'

There are Early English lancet windows in the east wall of the chancel, and Decorated windows in the chancel and nave. High on the south wall of the chancel is a pagan fertility figure, a shiela-na-gig. Some of the benches in the nave (Fig.152) are medieval, and the carved seventeenth-century family pew is notable, though somewhat damaged.

Access: From Craven Arms, take the B4368 towards Much Wenlock, passing through Diddlebury and Munslow. Half a mile after Munslow, turn right, then left, then right again, then left again for Holdgate.

St Martin, St Martin's

THIS church is worth visiting largely for its excellent roofs and woodwork. The structure of the church is a great hotchpotch of styles, but the overall result is successful, especially as seen from the south. The chancel is basically Early English, though the east wall and window were rebuilt in 1862. The south doorway is probably Decorated. The nave is separated from the north aisle by a Perpendicular

(Fig 153) **St Martin, St. Martin's** *Interior looking east.*

(Fig 154) **St Martin, St Martin's** *Three-decker pulpit.*

arcade (Fig.153), the eastern bays of which are earlier than the western. The windows in the south wall of the nave and chancel are late Perpendicular insertions. The tower is also late Perpendicular, and may be as late as 1632.

The nave roof is made of collar-beams on arched braces, with queen-posts giving additional support. The chancel roof is boarded, giving the effect of a wagon-roof (Fig.153); there is some carved decoration. Unfortunately, the previous set of box-pews has gone, the ends of the pews now panelling the east wall of the chancel. The show-piece of the church is the complete three-decker pulpit (Fig.154) now standing at the west end of the building. Though assembled only in 1810, some Jacobean pieces were re-used. On the south wall of the nave hangs a fine wooden carving (St Catherine) which is said to be Celtic.

Access: From Oswestry, proceed north along A438, until the road joins the new A5. Continue along the A5 for a short distance, then turn right for Gobowen; the B5069 will then take you to St Martin's. Just past the school, a road on the right leads to the church.

St George, Clun

CLUN, in the far south-west of the county, is, as one would expect, a most attractive little town set in scenery remote and tranquil. Yet its present peacefulness conceals a turbulent history as a border settlement, which changed hands repeatedly between the English and the Welsh in the Middle Ages. After the Norman Conquest, the de Say family held Clun from Earl Roger until 1155 when following the marriage of Isabel de Say to William Fitzalan it fell into the hands of the family who already held the lordship of Oswestry. A new town appears to have been built on the north bank of the river near the castle by the Fitzalans around 1200, there being also a pre-existing village around the church of St George on the south bank (Trinder). In 1233 the Welsh leader Llewellyn ap Iorwerth burnt Oswestry and Clun and occupied Shrewsbury; the Welsh were finally cleared from the border areas by Edward I in 1282-83.

The parish church of St George is set prominently halfway up the hill on the south side of the packhorse bridge over the river Clun. The church is of Norman origin, the oldest part probably dating from the mid-twelfth century. Note that the easternmost arch in the north arcade is rounded (Fig.155), all the others being pointed (i.e. late Norman or Transitional). The piers are rounded, short and sturdy, and are surmounted by square multi-scalloped capitals. The tower is also Norman (Fig.59, p26), a little later than the west wall of the nave, for a window in this wall looks into the tower. The tower is remarkable in that, like Hopesay and More, it has a double pyramid roof. The clerestory, on the south side only, has Norman windows above the piers. The roofs, both of the nave

(Fig 155) **St George, Clun** *North arcade. The easternmost arch is rounded, the others pointed.*

Left: (Fig 156) **St George, Clun** *Jacobean pulpit with tester.*

and the north aisle, comprise collar-beams on arched braces, with tiers of wind-braces forming quatre-foil patterns. The fine Jacobean pulpit (Fig.156) has its original tester (sounding-board) above.

Access: Clun is on the B4368 about ten miles west of Craven Arms. On entering the town, follow the A488 south towards Knighton, crossing the medieval bridge over the river. St George's is sited prominently on the left-hand side up the hill.

St Mary, Neen Savage

NEENTON, Neen Savage and Neen Sollars are all situated on the river Rea, and Neen was the former (British) name for the river (cf. Nene in Northamptonshire). Savage and Solariis were the surnames of the respective feudal owners in the twelfth and thirteenth centuries.

The church at Neen Savage (Fig.157) is attractively situated and is basically a late Norman building, consisting of nave, chancel and west tower. Norman round-headed windows persist in the chancel and nave; other windows are Early English (plate tracery) or late Perpendicular insertions. The porch is half-timbered, and is also Perpendicular. The screen and roof are very good. The screen (Fig.158) is basically

(Fig 157) **St Mary, Neen Savage**

(Fig 158) **St Mary, Neen Savage** *The screen, with trussed-rafter roof above.*

(Fig 159 and 160) **St Mary, Cleobury Mortimer** *Early English arcades, note the contrast between the Norman tower arch (Fig 159) and the Early English chancel arch (Fig 160).*

fifteenth or early sixteenth century, and has been much repaired, but it is very pretty. The roof (Fig.44, p22), of trussed rafters and tie-beams, contains some very ancient timbers. In the north wall of the chancel are two aumbries or recesses which were used to store the vessels used in the Eucharist.

Access: From Cleobury Mortimer (qv), take the B4363 north towards Bridgnorth; after one mile, turn left for Neen Savage; the church is on the left after half a mile.

St Mary, Cleobury Mortimer

THE elegant church and spire of St Mary's dominates the high street of this attractive south Shropshire town, which take the second part of its name from one of the great Marcher families. In Saxon times, Cleobury was in the possession of Queen Edith, wife of Edward the Confessor, and it passed to Ralph de Mortimer after the Norman Conquest The Mortimers took their family name from Mortimer in

St Andrew, Shifnal
(Fig 161) *Tower and south facade.*

Above: (Fig 162) *The nave looking east.*

Below: (Fig 163) *Early English north arcade.*

Opposite, top: (Fig 164) *South arcade with the upper storey of the porch extending above the south aisle.*

Opposite, bottom: (Fig 165) *The fine Decorated east window of the chancel.*

France, and they became based at Wigmore Castle in Herefordshire, which was also in the hands of Ralph. Later in the Middle Ages, they became one of the most powerful families in the realm: a descendant Roger Mortimer gained possession of Ludlow Castle and became enamoured of Queen Isabella, wife of Edward II. Together they overthrew the king, who was murdered in Berkeley Castle in 1327. They governed the country for a short time during Edward III's minority, but once the young king took power, Mortimer's days were numbered, and he was put to death in 1330; he founded the north chapel in Cleobury Mortimer's church.

The base of the tower is late Norman, and the tower arch (Fig.159) at the west end of the nave is round and somewhat depressed. The tower is surmounted by a lovely shingled broach-spire (Fig.69, p29), which is not quite symmetrical when seen from certain viewpoints. The rest of the church is basically Early English, dating from various periods in the thirteenth century. The fine south porch has a holy-water stoup, one of fewer than ten remaining in Shropshire. In the first half of the thirteenth century, the south aisle and chancel were built; the aisle has lancet windows, and the arcade of five bays has circular piers and capitals. The chancel arch (Fig.160) is very fine, and has three orders of shafts with stiff-leaf capitals. The north arcade (Fig.13,

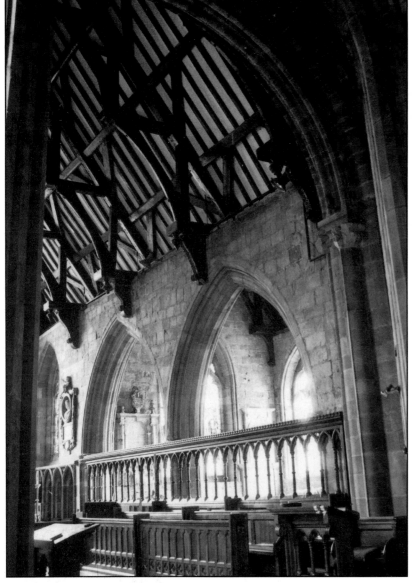

(Fig 166) *Double hammer-beam roof of the chancel.*

Although the main part of the church is Early English (thirteenth century), there are remains of the earlier Norman church. These are revealed by the semicircular arches of the late Norman period which may be seen in the chancel arch, the arch leading from the south transept into the south chancel chapel, the doorway in the south wall of the south transept, and the window in this transept now looking into the aisle.

In the thirteenth century, the nave, aisles and later the crossing tower were built in the Early English style, with Gothic arches supported by octagonal columns (Figs.162 and 163). Most remarkable is the two-storeyed porch (Fig.16, p14) which juts into the south aisle (Fig.164); the upper storey was probably first a priest's chamber and later a school.

In the Decorated period (fourteenth century) the chancel was rebuilt and is notable for the lovely east window (Fig.165) which has just recently been restored. A south chapel was added to the chancel at this time and this has a less elaborate reticulated east window. Outside this chapel is a tomb-recess with an ogee-headed canopy. Perpendicular windows were inserted in the next century in the north transept and the south aisle. The fine hammer-beam roofs of the nave and chancel (Fig.166) probably date from the end

p13) and north chapel date from the second half of the thirteenth century. The roofs are medieval; trussed rafters in the chancel, and collar-beams and wind-braces in the nave.

Access: The town is about midway between Ludlow and Kidderminster. Take the A4117 eastwards from Ludlow, and go over Cleehill; St Mary's is on the left side of the main street in the town.

of the sixteenth century after damage from the fire in Shifnal in 1591.

Access: Shifnal is five miles east of Telford. Leave the M54 at Exit 4; or alternatively from the A5, the B4379 leads to the town. St Andrew's is at the south-western edge of Shifnal not far from the road leading to Bridgnorth.

St Andrew, Shifnal

THE magnificence of St Andrew's church (Fig.161) undoubtedly dates from Shifnal's importance as an ecclesiastical centre in Saxon and Norman times. It was the collegiate church of an extensive Saxon parish which included Kemberton and Ryton, Dawley and Sheriffhales. In the Domesday Book it was known as Iteshale (later becoming Idshall). The college ceased some time after the Norman Conquest, and the church was acquired by Shrewsbury Abbey.

St Mary, Acton Burnell

ACTON means 'dwelling by the oak' and there are four Actons in Shropshire, three of which are distinguished by the surnames of the holders of the manor. In the Domesday Book, 'Actune' was held by Roger FitzCorbet, a member of the family of great Marcher lords who built Caus castle in the west of the county. The Burnells came on the scene one hundred years later, the earliest reference being to Gerin Burnell in 1183. One hundred years after this, one of the Burnells, Robert, rose to national importance, being Lord Chancellor of England under

(Fig 167) **St Mary, Acton Burnell** *with the castle ruins beyond.*

Edward I and Bishop of Bath and Wells. Parliament met in Acton Burnell in 1283, and in the next year Bishop Burnell obtained a licence to fortify the castle whose impressive ruins stand to the north of the church (Fig.167).

Meanwhile, St Mary's was being built, the date usually assigned to it being *c.*1270. It is justly celebrated for it was all built in one phase, towards the end of the Early English period. The eminence of its benefactor is reflected in the elegance of the building. Construction probably started at the west end, where there is a simple lancet window of three lights without tracery (Fig.167); compare this with the gorgeous detail of the east window of the chancel, which Pevsner describes as follows: 'east window of four lights, or rather two separate two-light windows with trefoiled circles set so closely that a larger cinquefoiled circle over both the trefoiled circles creates the impression of one wide and high window.' This was probably erected at the end of the Early English period – we are almost on the threshold of Decorated tracery. Note the Purbeck marble shafts of the chancel windows, and the double piscina with shafts and stiff-leaf capitals. In the south transept is a recess surmounted by an ogee-shaped canopy (Fig.18, p15); it no longer contains an effigy. There are medieval tiles on the floor of the north transept, and some notable monuments here: the finest brass in Shropshire commemorates Sir Nicholas Burnell (d.1382). In the sixteenth century, the manor was

(Fig 168) **St Mary, Acton Burnell** *Monument to Sir Richard Lee (1591).*

acquired by the Lees and the ornate tomb to Sir Richard Lee (d.1591, Fig.168) is held to rank with the Blount memorial in Kinlet church as the best of the Elizabethan monuments in the county. A further monument to Sir Humphrey Lee (d.1632) is also very fine. At the west end of the church, the Early English font is notable (Fig.169).

(Fig 169) **St Mary, Acton Burnell** *Early English font.*

Access: From Shrewsbury, follow A49 south past Dorrington and then after 1½ miles turn left to Longnor. Half a mile past Longnor village, turn left again along the old Roman road past Frodesley to reach Acton Burnell. The church is to the right of the hall (now a school).

St Mary, Longnor

THE manor of Longnor dates from the twelfth century, and the church was built one hundred years later as a chapel subordinate to Condover.

(Fig 170) **Longnor church.**

In the Middle Ages, the church was adjacent to the manor house, the original site of which can be seen as a mound under the trees near the south end of the church. The ubiquitous Corbets took over the manor in the fifteenth century, and in the seventeenth century the surrounding village was cleared to provide a suitable setting of their new hall which was built in 1670. The Corbets destroyed or moved other villages for parks at Acton Reynald, Moreton Corbet and Adderley.

Thanks to such clearances, St Mary's is now attractively situated overlooking the grounds of Longnor Hall. It is a lovely, simple, peaceful Early English church, less cluttered if less grand than Acton Burnell, its close contemporary. It was built *c.*1260-70, a date confirmed by the style of the windows. The tracery of the east window (very similar to that of Acton Burnell) has three lancets surmounted by three uncusped circles (Fig.170) – an indication that the Early English style would soon give way to Decorated. Plain lancet windows are grouped asymmetrically in the nave. The fittings inside are those of the eighteenth century unmodified – west gallery, box-pews, squire's pew, reader's desk and pulpit (Fig.171). The roof is of trussed rafters, plain and original (Fig.42, p22).

(Fig 171) **Longnor** *Box-pews and west gallery.*

Access: From Shrewsbury, proceed south along A49; 1½ miles after Dorrington, turn left to Longnor, and the church is on the right after about a quarter of a mile.

St Michael and All Angels, Alberbury

IN SAXON times there was a collegiate church here, and before the Norman Conquest the manor was held by the king, Edward the Confessor. After 1066, it passed (of course) to Earl Roger, and to Roger Fitz Corbet (of nearby Caus Castle) from him. By 1148 the church had been given to Shrewsbury Abbey; but in 1221-26 an Augustinian (later Grandmontine) priory was founded here, the church being appropriated by the priory in 1259. The priory ruins are now part of White Abbey Farm, situated 1½ miles from the church on the bank of the river Severn. In 1441, the church was given to All Souls College, Oxford, who retain the advowson to the present day.

The earliest and perhaps the most impressive part of the church is the Early English tower, built towards the end of the thirteenth century; the Decorated windows are later insertions. The tower is situated unusually at the north-east corner of the nave, and is surmounted by a steep saddleback roof, unique in Shropshire (Fig.172).

The south, or Loton, chapel was built about 40 years later in the Decorated manner, by the same family (the Corbets) who built the south aisle at Moreton Corbet; both chapels have an almost identical and most unusual west window in the form of a large spheric triangle. The windows of the south

(Fig 172) **St Michael, Alberbury**

wall of the chapel are in the Decorated manner, and the arcade is supported by piers of quatrefoil section.

The nave was largely reconstructed in Victorian times, but is notable for the very fine ancient roof – one of the best in Shropshire. There are collar-beams on arched braces, with five tiers of wind-braces arranged in quatrefoil patterns.

Access: From Shrewsbury, take the Welshpool road (A458) westwards for about six miles; then fork right on to the B4394 signposted Llandrinio. Alberbury is three miles along this road, the church being down a short lane on the right.

St John the Baptist, Hughley

ALTHOUGH one visits Hughley essentially to see the screen (the finest in Shropshire), there is in fact a good deal else to admire.

The earliest part of the church is the Early English thirteenth-century north wall of the nave, with its lancet windows. The rest of the church was built towards the end of the Decorated period, c.1360. In the chancel, the east window shows curvilinear tracery, and there are fragments of medieval stained

(Fig 173, 174, 175 and 176) **St John the Baptist, Hughley** *The screen, the finest in Shropshire.*

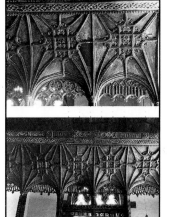

glass here and in the north window. To the right of the altar is a corbel projecting in the form of a lady's head (Fig.176), and in the south wall a pillar piscina. In the nave there are medieval tiles on the floor, and an excellent boarded trussed-rafter roof.

But the quality of the Perpendicular screen (Fig. 173) dwarfs all else. Cranage describes it: 'The original part of the cornice (the upper section) is very beautiful (Fig. 174) and has carvings of birds, grapes and flowers. Below this is a band of wavy quatrefoils, and then a coved surface, ornamented with ribs and panels. The tracery under the eight arches is extremely varied: the two central divisions rest on another arch of more depressed character.' The upper part of the dado (lower part of the screen (Fig.176) is also delicately carved. Vallance (in *English Church Screens*) comments that in the vaulting of the screen, exquisite effects are produced by the disposition of the ribs in stellar plan (Fig.174), and cites similar examples at Astbury (Cheshire), Denbigh and Gresford (North Wales) and Aymestrey (Herefordshire).

Access: From Much Wenlock, take the B4371 south-west towards Church Stretton along Wenlock Edge; the turning to Hughley falls away quite steeply to the right after four miles, and the church is in the village on the right.

(Fig 177) **St Peter, Chelmarsh**

St Peter, Chelmarsh

ST PETER'S, Chelmarsh (Fig.177) is, perhaps, the best example of Decorated architecture in Shropshire, for, apart from the Norman south doorway and the Georgian tower (1720), the building is entirely in that style. This gives it a unity internally which is very appealing. The north arcade (Fig.178) has four bays, with octagonal piers surmounted by capitals with ball-flower ornamentation (Fig.21, p16). The fine east window (Fig.178) is very similar to those at Kinlet and Stottesdon (q.v.). The windows in the nave each have two tall lights with a little chaste Decorated tracery above. The roof consists of curved trussed rafters.

(Fig 178) **St Peter, Chelmarsh** *The Decorated arcade and east window.*

Access: From Bridgnorth take the B4555 south for about four miles. St Peter's is on the left.

St Peter, Worfield

WORFIELD is a pretty village on the river Worfe, and the tower and spire of St Peter's is a landmark for miles around; the tower is 80 feet high, and the spire (the finest in Shropshire) 120 feet (Fig.71, p30).

There was apparently a Norman and Early English church here, but only a few traces remain, the bulk of the church as we see it today dating from the fourteenth century. Earliest is the chancel, followed by the nave; this is separated from the aisles by a Decorated arcade of grand proportions. Later in the four-

(Fig 179) **St Peter, Worfield**

(Fig 180) **St Peter, Worfield**

(Fig 181) **St Mary Magdalene, Battlefield** *Perpendicular (left) and Decorated windows side by side.*

(Fig 182) **St Mary Magdalene, Battlefield** *Screen and chancel, with the Pietà on the north wall.*

teenth century, at the beginning of the Perpendicular period, came the tower and spire (Figs 179 and 180). The window at the east end of the north aisle is very fine. There is a fifteenth-century font, a partly original Perpendicular screen, and two elaborate Elizabethan tombs at the west end of the north aisle.

Access: From Bridgnorth, take the A454 towards Wolverhampton. The village is four miles away, on the left.

St Mary Magdalene, Battlefield

BATTLEFIELD is unusual among medieval churches because it can be precisely dated, the body of the church being built in 1406-08. The battle of Shrewsbury occurred on 21 July, 1403 between the rebel forces of Henry Percy (Hotspur) in

alliance with others including the Welsh leader Owain Glyndwr and those of the king, Henry IV; it ended with the defeat of the rebels and the death of Hotspur, immortalised by Shakespeare in Henry IV Part I. Casualties were high, and 1,600 bodies were buried at the site of the battle.

The local rector, Roger Ive, obtained a licence from the king for land for the foundation of a chapel where prayers could be said for the dead and mass celebrated daily. The king granted a foundation charter which created a perpetual chantry, with a college consisting of a Master and six chaplains. This lasted until the Reformation, when chantries were suppressed and the college was dissolved in 1548. The church then became a parish church, but suffered severe neglect in the eighteenth century when the roof of the nave collapsed; it was not restored until 1861.

The church (Fig.183) is quite isolated at the end of a lane, shielded from the busy outside world by the Shrewsbury-Crewe railway embankment. On a recent visit in May, the bird-song was entrancing, and the churchyard was gay with cowslips and violets, bluebells and primroses. The nave was built in the first decade of the fifteenth century, and it is striking and very unusual to see adjacent windows, built at the same time, in the Decorated and Perpendicular styles (Fig.181) – a classic example of how medieval styles of building may overlap, and a warning against the too rigid separation of building periods beloved by some antiquaries. The fine Perpendicular tower was built

(Fig 183) **St Mary Magdalene, Battlefield**

later in the fifteenth or early in the sixteenth century.

Internally the church is spacious and dignified, and consists of nave and chancel without aisles. The hammer-beam roof is fine (Fig.51, p24) and dates from the Victorian restoration, as does the screen (Fig.182). In the chancel is a marvellous wooden Pietà dating from the early fifteenth century. In the vestry are interesting exhibits relating to the battle of Shrewsbury and some medieval stained glass.

Access: From Shrewsbury, take the A49 north; about 250 yards after the A53 branches to the right, an unmarked lane leads on the left under a railway bridge, and the church is a little beyond. It was closed for services in 1982, and is now in the care of the Redundant Churches Fund. It is open on Sundays in May to August, 2-5pm, or by arrangement with the vicar.

St Mary and St Bartholomew, Tong

TONG church is large and impressive when seen from afar, and closer inspection does not diminish the impact. for this miniature cathedral houses one of the finest series of medieval tombs in the country; in parish churches, only Harewood and Macclesfield have more alabaster effigies than Tong (Gardner); and the building is a fit

(Fig 184) *Stalls in the chancel.*

St Mary and St Bartholomew, Tong
(Fig 185) *View from the south.*

receptacle for this portrayal of the aristocracy in heaven.

The manor of Tong is described in the Domesday Book as 'Tuange' (a fork in the river) and was held by Earl Roger. He gave the church to the newly-founded Shrewsbury Abbey. The manor passed through various owners in the early Middle Ages, and then fell into the hands of the Pembrugge family.

(Fig 186) *Fan-vaulting in the Vernon chapel (1515).*

(Fig 187) *Monument to Sir Fulke de Pembrugge and Dame Isabella (1446).*

After the death of Sir Fulke de Pembrugge in 1409, the church was rebuilt by his widow Isabella, who founded a chantry college whose members would say mass daily for the soul of her husband and those of her two previous husbands.

The church thus dates from the early years of the fifteenth century, only part of the south arcade remaining from the previous Early English building. Externally, the church is battlemented and pinnacled, and has a central tower, square below and octagonal above surmounted by a short spire (Fig.185). Inside, the Perpendicular arcades are supported by tall, octagonal columns. The roof of the nave is low-pitched, with arched braces and finely carved bosses. The chancel (Fig.184) is richly furnished with stalls for the members of the college and under the seats are a fine set of misericords. To the south is the Vernon chapel, which was added in 1515 as chantry chapel by Sir Henry Vernon; it has exquisite fan-vaulting (Fig.186), a rare feature in a parish church.

But then Tong is no ordinary church: for the series of tombs is spectacular. A group of seven tombs below the chancel steps and extending into the Vernon chapel comprise a treasure of national importance. It begins with the tomb of the foundress, Lady Isabella, with her husband, 1446 (Fig.187); and proceeds with those of the Vernon family of Haddon Hall, Derbyshire. (Sir Richard Vernon inherited Tong from his great-uncle, Lady Isabella's husband.) In chronological order the tombs are as follows: 1446, Lady Isabella de Pembrugge (alabaster); 1451, Sir Richard Vernon (alabaster; Fig.188) (he wears the SS collar, a livery collar of the House of Lancaster, probably instituted by John of Gaunt in the late fourteenth century); 1467, Sir William Vernon; 1515, Sir Henry Vernon (Fig.189); 1517, Richard Vernon (alabaster); 1542, Humphrey Vernon; 1546, Sir Thomas Stanley (who married a daughter of Sir George Vernon). It is fascinating to observe the changes in fashion as the sequence progresses to and beyond the end of the Middle Ages. Finally, in the south chapel, is a fine wall-bust commemorating Sir Arthur Vernon (died 1516), youngest son of Sir Henry Vernon.

Access: Tong is just half a mile north of the intersection of the A41 and M54 (exit 3).

Above: (Fig 188) *Monument to Sir Richard Vernon and his wife (1451).*

(Fig 189) *Monument to Sir Henry Vernon and his wife (1515); beyond is the Stanley tomb (1576)*

St Laurence, Ludlow

WE HAVE seen how seldom church building in the Perpendicular age in Shropshire extended to anything more than a tower. Why, then, does the church of St Laurence, stand out as so great an exception? – for as an example of Perpendicular elegance it can stand comparison with any other church in the country. The answer must lie in the much greater prosperity of Ludlow, and in particular of the Palmers' Guild, in contrast to the relatively straitened circumstances of the rest of the county.

Ludlow does not appear in the Domesday Book, and the town appears to have been founded shortly after the building of the castle in 1085 by Roger de Lacy. It is thought that a market centre grew up in the shadow of the castle (Platt), and the town developed as a deliberate Norman plantation (Rowley). At the time of the Domesday survey (1087) Ludlow was part of the manor of Stanton Lacy (q.v.) where there was a Saxon church.

St Laurence, Ludlow
(Fig 190) *The tower.*

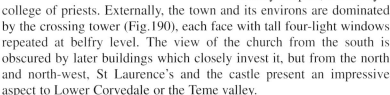

Left, top: (Fig 191) *The nave looking east.* Left, middle upper: (Fig 192) *Vaulting above the crossing.* Left, middle lower and bottom: (Fig 193 and 194) *Misericords.* Below: (Fig 195) *Monument to Edward Waties (1635).*

St Laurence's, the largest parish church in Shropshire, started as a small Norman church in the twelfth century, and appears to have been rebuilt at the very end of that century, in 1199. Only vestigial remains survive of that rebuilding – Pevsner cites a flat buttress east of the porch, another in the south chancel chapel, and a round-headed recess in the same chapel. In the thirteenth century, the fine south doorway was built, and the hexagonal porch dates from the early part of the fourteenth century. There is only one other such porch in England – at St Mary Redcliffe, Bristol. Also in the fourteenth century, the north aisle was built in Decorated style. The windows of this aisle show much ball-flower decoration – the four-light west window, and the six two-

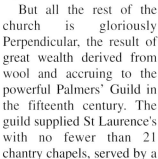

light windows in the north wall.

But all the rest of the church is gloriously Perpendicular, the result of great wealth derived from wool and accruing to the powerful Palmers' Guild in the fifteenth century. The guild supplied St Laurence's with no fewer than 21 chantry chapels, served by a college of priests. Externally, the town and its environs are dominated by the crossing tower (Fig.190), each face with tall four-light windows repeated at belfry level. The view of the church from the south is obscured by later buildings which closely invest it, but from the north and north-west, St Laurence's and the castle present an impressive aspect to Lower Corvedale or the Teme valley.

Inside, the arcades of the nave are tall Perpendicular (Fig.191), with wide aisles, a clerestory, and a low-pitched roof with tie-beams and carved bosses. Towards the west end of the north aisle is an impressive canopied recess, of unknown dedication. Screens separate the north and south aisles from the north and south chapels, and the nave from the chancel, the north screen being the finest. The north and east windows of the north chapel contain some good medieval stained glass. Looking upwards (at the risk of dislocating one's neck), the vaulting over the crossing is very impressive (Fig.192). The chancel is dominated by the tremendous height of the Perpendicular windows, and houses a fine set of choir-stalls dating from 1447. Under the seats are an excellent series of misericords (Figs.193 and 194), with carvings amusing, irreverent and grotesque.

There are some notable monuments in the north chapel, the chancel, and the south transept; that to Edward Waties is illustrated (Fig.195).

Access: St Laurence's is in the centre of Ludlow, and literally cannot be missed.

St Peter, Edgmond

THE overall impression of St Peter's is that of a late Perpendicular church, a rarity in Shropshire: built of red sandstone, it is in fact the nearest parallel in Shropshire to the Perpendicular churches for which Cheshire is well-known. The church is nicely situated, with the path through the well-kept churchyard leading to the fine porch. Beyond is the tower, and battlements on the roof of the tower and nave confirm the Perpendicular origin of the building. A glance to the right, at the chancel, however, immediately reveals that all is not of one

Above: (Fig 196) **St Peter, Edgmond** *Perpendicular tower and south aisle; Decorated chancel.*

Left: (Fig 198) **St Peter, Edgmond** *The font.*

(Fig 197) **St Peter, Edgmond** *Nave and chancel.*

period; for there are clear Decorated windows contrasting with the Perpendicular windows of the south aisle (Fig.196).

Internally, again, the impression is of a Perpendicular building which, on closer inspection, reveals remains of earlier work. The tall, slender octagonal columns of the Perpendicular arcades (Fig.197) separate the nave from the aisles; but the bases of the columns are round, and, as Cranage pointed out, are the remains of an earlier Early English arcade. He also noted that the eastern respond (the half-column bonded into the wall carrying the easternmost arch) is circular, not octagonal, and that the lower part of this was also part of the earlier arcade.

As already mentioned, the chancel is Decorated,

with an east window showing curvilinear tracery, a double piscina in the south wall, and a fine brass in the north-east corner. The excellent font is the oldest object in the church, being early Norman (Fig.198); it is ornamented with cable, interlacing and other patterns and probably dates from the time soon after the Norman conquest when Earl Roger of Montgomery gave Edgmond to the monks of Shrewsbury Abbey.

Access: Edgmond is two miles west of Newport. Take the former A41 out of Newport, and turn left into B5062 (signposted Shrewsbury); after half a mile, the road to Edgmond is on the left.

St Peter, Melverley

MELVERLEY means 'grove by the mill ford', and, according to the church guide, in Saxon times the manor was held by a man named Ealric. In the Domesday Book, 'Melevrlei' was said to be held by Sheriff Rainald from Earl Roger of Montgomery. Ordericus Vitalis (see Atcham) in his

(Fig 199) **St Peter, Melverley**

(Fig 200) **St Peter, Melverley** *Interior from the chancel.*

(Fig 201) **Halston chapel** *Pews, panelling and pulpit.*

(Fig 202) **Halston chapel** *Gallery and candelabra.*

Historia Ecclesiastica mentions a wooden church on the banks of the river near Shrewsbury, which is thought to be an earlier building which was destroyed by Owain Glyndwr in 1401. Apparently the church was immediately rebuilt, and was said to be in use by 1406. This dates fits well with Cranage's conclusion that the present building is fifteenth century (or even fourteenth century, he adds at one point): timbered buildings are notoriously difficult to date.

'Black-and-white' churches are undoubtedly both rare and quaint, and Melverley is no exception. St Peter's stands precariously near the east bank of the river Vyrnwy near its confluence with the Severn (Fig.199). Its foundations were seriously threatened by flooding in February 1990, and at the time of writing extensive works are in progress to protect the church from further hazard.

Most half-timbered dwellings in Shropshire are sixteenth century or later, and the narrowness of the wattle-and-daub between the vertical timbers is consistent with the earlier date given for St Peter's. Internally, there is a west gallery sloping to the south, and reached by a rickety flight of stairs. The plain screen divides the nave and chancel, and is connected vertically with one of the tie-beams of the roof (Fig.200).

Access: Melverley is signposted from the A5 1½ miles east from Nesscliffe. On reaching the village, turn left and soon afterwards a short lane on the right leads to the church.

Halston Chapel

THIS chapel in the grounds of Halston Hall is not, and so far as I know, never has been a parish church, but it demands inclusion in any book on Shropshire churches because of the quality and rarity of its furnishings.

After the Norman conquest, Halston manor was held from Earl Roger by Rainald the sheriff, according to the Domesday Book (1087), but by the middle of the twelfth century it had come into the hands of the Knights of St John of Jerusalem, who owned it until

the Dissolution. By 1551, it belonged to the Mytton family, but was briefly restored to the Knights by Queen Mary. Elizabeth confirmed the Myttons in their ownership, and it remained with this family for 300 years. The original Hospitallers' preceptory was probably adjacent to the site of the present chapel, but in 1690 the Myttons moved their dwelling to drier ground 400 yards away when the present Halston Hall was built, and the preceptory was demolished.

So the chapel stands alone in pleasant parkland, surrounded by yews. There is an incongruous eighteenth-century brick tower, but the remainder of the building is half-timbered and very attractive to the modern eye. When was it built? No one knows, and previous guesses have ranged from the late fourteenth to the mid-sixteenth centuries. Modern opinion seems cautiously to be converging on a later date, making Halston, like Langley, an Elizabethan chapel – a great rarity.

But nice though the exterior undoubtedly is, it is the interior which is truly breathtaking because of the remarkable range of Elizabethan and Jacobean fittings. The pews are displayed facing each other, as in a college chapel, with panelling on both sides and at the east end (Fig.201). The two-decker pulpit is later, dated 1725. The west gallery (Fig.202), bearing the Hanoverian Royal Arms, is carried by the westernmost tie-beam. The roof-trusses are moulded and the spandrels carved with various figures, including a bishop. There is a fine brass chandelier carrying candles (electricity is not installed), and family hatchments adorn the north and south walls.

Langley Chapel

AMONG Shropshire churches, there is no greater contrast than to move from Tong, with its opulent memorials to the nobility of the fifteenth and sixteenth centuries, to Langley, where the humble Puritans worshipped. Barely fifty years separate some of the tombs of Tong from the plain benches of Langley, yet what an upheaval of religious belief is implied. There can be no clear illustration of what the Reformation was all about. I am indebted to English Heritage for permission to reproduce the following account of Langley chapel:

'There had been a chapel at Langley in the Middle Ages, but the existing building was probably erected in late Tudor times. At that period Langley Hall, whose ruins are in the farm nearby, was in active use and there was sufficient congregation to need this chapel. The disappearance of the hall and the shrinkage of the local population led to the gradual disuse and abandonment of the building as a place of worship in the first half of the last century. After many years of neglect it was placed in the care of the Office of Works in 1915. The main interest in the chapel lies in the fact that its fittings and furnishings, normally replaced in other churches and chapels in the eighteenth and nineteenth centuries, because of its early and gradual abandonment, have been left largely undisturbed and so reveal the arrangements within the seventeenth-century puritan church. The chapel, which has no known dedication, is a simple rectangular building with a three-light window at the east end and two doors on the south aisle. The chancel is not a separate structure, but its floor, paved with re-used medieval tiles, is slightly raised above that of the nave, and the demarcation is emphasised by a massive moulded tie-beam with roofs of different construction on either side of it – collar-braced in the nave (Fig.203) and trussed rafters in the chancel.

'One of the columns in the nave has the date 1601 carved in it, while the initials on this and elsewhere probably belong to carpenters. On the south side of the nave, decorated plasterwork is seen; originally this was on both sides. At the west end is a wooden bellcote. It is not certain that the wooden furniture is the same date as the roof of 1601, but it is not later than the early decades of the seventeenth century. Altars had been removed from some English churches by the mid-sixteenth century, and in 1603 it was laid down that every church should have a pulpit and a reading desk. At Langley the pulpit stands on the

south side and the reading desk on the north by the chancel step. The reading desk has seats on two sides, but has lost its lectern and sounding-board. In the nave are box-pews at the east end and rudely hewn benches behind them (Fig.204). The arrangements in the chancel are most interesting from a liturgical point of view.

(Fig 203) **Langley Chapel** *Roof with tie-beams and collar-beams on arched braces.*

(Fig 204) **Langley Chapel** *Interior showing the seventeenth-century furnishings.*

The communion table is still well forward with benches and kneeling desks originally on the north, east and south sides, but now only surviving incompletely. The strictest Puritans would have had provision for kneeling on the west side also, and the fact that it is open may reflect the views of the lord of the manor or may be a post-Restoration alteration.'

Access: Follow the instructions for Acton Burnell (p64). From there, proceed south along a lane to Ruckley; after 1¼ miles, a lane branches off to the left, and Langley chapel is about 300 yards along on the right.

St Mary and St Andrew, Condover

CONDOVER (meaning 'Bank of the river Cound') was a collegiate church in Saxon times, and after the Conquest was given by Earl Roger to Shrewsbury Abbey.

The present church is such a strange mixture of styles because the previous building largely fell down on 22 November 1660. Surviving from the medieval church, however, is the Norman north transept; in its north wall there are large windows with nook-shafts at the sides, with waterleaf capitals. More remarkable, however, is a rare Norman quatrefoil window set high in the north wall of the transept and deeply splayed internally. The nave was rebuilt in the reign of Charles II, a rare period for church building; perhaps the finest thing in the church is the roof which spans the exceedingly wide nave. This is a hammer-beam roof (Fig.205), with collar-beams on arched braces. Externally, the south transept has an engaging half-timbered gable. The chancel and north chapel (Fig.206) are Victorian, and house a remarkable series of monuments. These include Elizabethan (recumbent alabaster effigies of Thomas Scriven and his wife – 1587), Stuart (two pairs of seventeenth-century

(Fig.205) **St Mary and St Andrew, Condover** *Nave with the fine seventeenth-century hammer-beam roof.*

(Fig 206) **St Mary and St Andrew, Condover** *Statue of Sir Thomas Cholmondeley (1864); behind is the monument to Dame Jane Norton, with her husband, father and brother (1640).*

kneeling figures of Dame Jane Norton and her husband, and below her father Judge Owen and her brother) and Victorian (notably the kneeling figure of Sir Thomas Cholmondeley, died 1864, which quite dominates the eastern end of the church).

Access: Condover is five miles south of Shrewsbury. Proceed south along A49, and just past Bayston Hill fork left for Condover. Turn left in the village and the church is at the end of a short lane.

Holy Trinity, Minsterley

EYTON, the noted Shropshire antiquarian, states that there was a collegiate church here in Saxon times (as the name implies), later moved to Westbury, and the chapel of ease in Minsterley remained subordinate to West-bury until the present church was built in 1689. The building of Minsterley was a sharp break with the past in Shropshire: all the previous buildings and rebuildings harked back to the medieval past. Minsterley, in spite of the engaging oddities of the west facade, looks forward to the eighteenth century and beyond. It was the first church in the county to be built along Classical lines, and the first in which brick was used. As Pevsner points out, 1689 is a rare date for a church building.

The most striking aspect of the church is undoubtedly the west facade (Fig.207) topped by

(Fig 207) **Holy Trinity, Minsterley** *(1689).*

a weather-boarded belfry. At either side, giant segmented columns run from the base to the arched pediment above the clock. The west portal has a segmental arch, with a frieze above decorated with skulls and bones. An arched window above the portal is flanked by pilasters decked with garlands.

The interior is more sober in the Protestant tradition, with some fine original woodwork, notably the pulpit with large sounding-board, the communion rail, and the panelling of the chancel. There is a west gallery, above which is displayed a set of maidens' garlands. These eighteenth-century fancies were lovingly constructed in memory of young betrothed girls who died before their wedding-day.

Access: Minsterley is about 12 miles south-west of Shrewsbury, on the A488 Bishop's Castle road. In the village turn right along the road to Westbury, and the church is immediately on the left.

St Alkmund, Whitchurch

WHITCHURCH arose in Roman times as Mediolanum (the place in the middle of the plain) and was situated halfway along the road between what is now Wroxeter and Chester. In the Domesday Book it was known as Westune (indicating that it was on the western border of England), and it presumably acquired its present name after the construction of a Norman church in stone, possibly replacing a wooden Saxon predecessor.

The dedication to St Alkmund is unusual: Alkmund was the younger son of Alcred, King of Northumbria, and he died in battle in 822. St Alkmund's church in Shrewsbury was founded ninety years later by the formidable Aethelflaed, daughter of Alfred the Great, wife of Ethelred, king of Mercia, and known as the Lady of the Mercians. She captured Derby, where another dedication to St Alkmund exists, from the Danes; other churches with this dedication are at Aymestrey, Herefordshire, and Blyborough, Lincoln-shire (Revd. David Jenkins, in the excellent church guide).

Later in medieval times, the Norman church was extended, for according to a surviving picture there were Early English windows and finally a Perpendicular tower. Tower and church collapsed on Sunday, 31 July, 1711.

Now in Whitchurch is a very fine Queen Anne church, surpassing in elegance all the other eighteenth-century churches in Shropshire, with the possible exception of the much later St Chad's, Shrewsbury. It was built of red sandstone in eighteen months from March 1712. There is a large west tower with balustrade and pinnacles (Fig.208), and a semicircular south porch rebuilt exactly after the original in 1925. Inside, a fine staircase leads up to the west gallery; below there is a sense of space and dignity, with tall Tuscan columns and arches

(Fig 208) **St Alkmund, Whitchurch** *(1713)*

(Fig 209) **St Alkmund, Whitchurch** *The interior.*

separating the nave from the aisles (Fig.209). At the east end is the apse with three tall windows, and just to the south of this the Lady Chapel. This contains the fifteenth-century effigy of the renowned Sir John Talbot, earl of Shrewsbury, who fell in battle in 1453 in his eightieth year.

Access: At the north end of the High Street.

(Fig 210) **St Andrew, Quatt** *(1763)*

St Andrew, Quatt

THE derivation of Quatt and Quatford has given etymologists a deal of trouble. Quatt is a shortening of Quatton, and one theory is that the two names are the 'tun' (homestead) and ford of Cwatt (a personal name); alternatively, the first component may be OE Cwead – a muddy place.

Just as confusing at first sight is St Andrew's church, attractively situated opposite the magnificent eighteenth-century dower house. The church appears to be Georgian (Fig.210), and indeed the tower, nave and the wall of the north aisle were built of brick in 1763. But the chancel and north chapel are medieval.

(Fig 211) **St Andrew, Quatt** *Georgian nave with medieval north arcade.*

The former is not later than 1200, the priest's doorway in the south wall having a round-headed arch. The chancel windows and fine roof are Perpendicular. The chapel to the north of the chancel is Decorated, and the arcade separating the nave from the north aisle is probably also fourteenth century (Fig.211). The east end of the arcade is not, as usual, bonded into the wall by a corbel or respond, but terminates in a free-standing column, with what Cranage describes as a sort of flying buttress linking it to the chancel.

The font is Norman. The pulpit and reading-desk are inscribed 1629. There are a series of good monuments to the Wolryche family of nearby Dudmaston Hall (National Trust).

Access: From Bridgnorth, take the A442 south towards Kidderminster. Quatt is about five miles along this road; in the village, turn left into a short lane, and St Andrew's is on the right.

St Chad, Shrewsbury

IN Anglo-Saxon times, there were five parishes in Shrewsbury – those of Holy Cross, St Chad, St Alkmund, St Julian and St Mary; of the medieval churches, only Holy Cross and St Mary's remain. St Julian's, apart from the tower, was rebuilt in 1749-50; St Chad's fell down in 1788; and shortly after this scare, St Alkmund's was pulled down, again with the exception of the tower.

Old St Chad's was an Anglo-Saxon foundation, St

(Fig 212) **St Chad, Shrewsbury** *(1792) View from the south-east.*

Left and centre: (Fig 213 and 214) *The circular nave.* Right: (Fig 215) *The chancel.*

(Fig 216) *The ceiling.*

Chad being the first bishop of Mercia, making his episcopal seat at Lichfield; he died in 672, and was canonised in 779. It was a large cruciform church, originally collegiate, served by a Dean and a number of canons before the Reformation. The remains of the old church may still be seen in Princess Street. The new St Chad's was built in 1790-92 to the design of George Stuart, and the elegant church has a beautiful situation overlooking the park known as the Quarry and the broad sweep of the river Severn. The nave is circular, and in front is the entrance hall, with a stately portico of four tall Tuscan columns, with a pediment above (Fig.212). This is surmounted in turn by the square-based tower, and above this a circular colonnade, a cupola, and a golden cross.

Pevsner describes the interior as follows: 'The interior is a remarkable spatial experience. Three stages – a circular hall under the tower, the anteroom with the two apsed ends in which most elegantly two arms of a staircase sweep up to the gallery, their handrail being of thin simple iron shapes, and the nave or rotunda with its gallery three-quarters round, converting the circular room into a horse-shoe auditorium (Figs.213 and 214) and a separate chancel. The chancel is singled out by pairs of giant Corinthian columns placed behind one another and by a very large Venetian window (Fig.215). The gallery rests on short unfluted Ionic columns, and on these stand exceedingly attenuated Corinthian columns to support the flat ceiling (Fig.216).'

Access: Just to the west of the town centre, overlooking the Quarry.

(Fig 217) **St Margaret, Moreton Say** *(1788)*

St Margaret, Moreton Say

MORETON means the homestead ('tun') by the moor; the second component of the name, as is frequent in Shropshire, is from the local lords of the manor, the de Say family. They were originally from Sai in Normandy, and held the lordship of Clun after the Conquest; they gave their name also to Hopesay and Stokesay in the county.

At first sight, St Margaret's appears a typical Georgian church, and indeed the tower was built in Classical style in 1769, the same year as the tower in

(Fig 218) **St Margaret, Moreton Say** *View from the chancel.*

Moreton Corbet was completed in Perpendicular style. Built of warm red brick, the church appears to epitomise the end of the eighteenth century (Fig.217); but step inside, and the doorway at the west end of the nave leading to the base of the tower is clearly late Norman, and has been dated *c.*1190. So what happened in 1788, when the rest of the church was built, was that the medieval building was encased in brick.

Inside, the seventeenth century is at least as important as the eighteenth, largely due to Jane Vernon. In 1623, she erected a monument in the north wall of the chancel, where she is seen flanked by effigies of her two husbands. In 1634, she built the west gallery (Fig.218),one of the finest in Shropshire; and in 1642 a charming wooden memorial to three of her sisters was placed on the north wall of the chancel (Fig.219).

(Fig 219) **St Margaret, Moreton Say** *Monument to the three Vernon sisters (1642).*

Access: Moreton Say is four miles west of Market Drayton. Take the A53 towards Shrewsbury, and after two miles turn right into A41 at Ternhill. After one mile, a lane leads from the right to Moreton Say, and the church is in the village on the right side of the road.

St Michael, Llanyblodwel

ST Michael's has had a poor press from architectural historians. 'One cannot help smiling at the absurdity of Llanyblodwel', says Dean Cranage. 'Everything is incorrect here,' pronounces Pevsner a little loftily, 'and little is beautiful.' Perhaps so, but less eminent folk will derive a great deal of enjoyment from visiting Llanyblodwel; the setting of the tiny village is enchanting, with the old stone arched bridge over the river Tanat and the half-timbered Horseshoe Inn to admire, as well as the idiosyncratic St Michael's (Fig.220).

(Fig 220) **St Michael and All Angels, Llanyblodwel** *(altered 1850).*

Llanyblodwel was originally a medieval church, for there is a Norman south doorway, and a Perpendicular arcade separates the north aisle from the nave (Fig.221). The two east windows and part of the screen are also Perpendicular. By the 1840s, however, the south wall was becoming ruinous, and the vicar, the Reverend John Parker took a hand. He

(Fig 221) **St Michael and All Angels, Llanyblodwel** *Perpendicular arcade with Victorian decoration.*

built the octagonal west steeple, semi-detached from the church, and radically revised the interior. He designed the porch, ceiling, reredos, and dormer windows, and was responsible for the whole decor. Today, St Michael's stands as a memorial to a man of great ability and energy – and if he offended against the accepted canons of architectural design, so what!

Access: From Oswestry, proceed south along A483 towards Welshpool. After four miles, turn right at Llynclys along A495, and then fork right along B4396 towards Bala. After half a mile, the turning to Llanyblodwel is to the left. At the foot of the hill, the lane turns left over the Tanat, and the lane to the church is straight ahead, St Michael's being about 200 yards on the right.

(Figs 222 and 223) **All Saints, Batchcott** *(1892).*

All Saints, Batchcott (Richard's Castle)

THE last church in this series is the only one which can be called 'modern' even though it is now 100 years old. It was designed and built by Norman Shaw in 1891-1892, and is generally accepted as the best Victorian church in Shropshire. By the last decade of the century, the more flamboyant excesses of Victorianism were giving way to a plainer style heralding the advent of the twentieth century. The massive south-west tower stands away from the south aisle, and there is an imposing entrance adjacent to the tower. The church looks impressive as one walks along the yew-lined path from the south (Fig.222); and then one steps into a spacious and light-filled interior (Fig.223), with windows in the Decorated and Perpendicular styles. The chancel is dominated by the reredos painted as a medieval

triptych by Charles Buckeridge. The total effect is dignified and restrained.

Access: From Ludlow, proceed south along A49 for two miles, then turn right into B4361. The church is 1½ miles along this road, on the right.

Retrospect and Prospect

WE began this series in the eighth century and conclude it at the end of the nineteenth. What has our own century to offer? Pevsner, writing in 1958, found none, and I do not know of any churches built since then that ought to be included. There may be some, and I should be happy to receive readers' suggestions. It would be sad if, for the first time in a thousand years, a century had passed with nothing to offer. Perhaps the next one will do better!

Let Dean Cranage, the greatest authority on Shropshire's churches, have the last word:

'How does Shropshire compare with other counties in the beauty of its churches? One's natural partiality must not blind one to the fact that it is not in the first rank. It would be foolish to rate the churches so highly as those of a county like Lincoln. The Norman work is surpassed in some of the home counties, the Early English in Northamptonshire, the Decorated in Oxfordshire, the Perpendicular in Norfolk and Suffolk. The towers are nothing to those of Somersetshire; the spires are few; splendid fonts are rare; vaulting is almost non-existent; roofs are surpassed in East Anglia, screens in Devonshire, rood lofts in Wales, pulpits, stalls, bench ends in several other counties. But, in these remarks, I am speaking of the county as a whole and not of individual churches. The tower of Ludlow, the spire of Worfield, the font at Stottesdon, the fan-vaulting at Tong, stand out as of the first importance, as do such roofs as those at Alberbury, Clun, Condover, and St Mary's Shrewsbury, and such screens and stalls as those of Ludlow, to say nothing of many another feature which might be singled out. Indeed, many churches in Shropshire are worthy to be compared with the best elsewhere. For the church as a whole or for some large portion the following are quite deserving of the front rank:- Acton Burnell, Chelmarsh, Edstaston, Kinlet, Ludlow, Shrewsbury (Holy Cross and St Mary), Tong. Many an artist would add the views of Atcham and Melverley with the Severn (sic) in front of them, of Ellesmere from the south-east, of the cross at Bitterley, to say nothing of the glorious scenery with which so many of the churches are associated.'

Glossary

Abacus: a flat slab above a capital.

Advowson: the right of presentation of a priest to a church.

Apse: the semicircular or polygonal end of the chancel.

Arcade: a range of arches supported by piers or columns.

Arch: curved supporting structure, made of wedge-shaped sections.

Arched brace: see *Roof.*

Aumbry: a recess or cupboard to hold the vessels for Mass or Communion.

Ball-flower: Ornamentation used in the Decorated period consisting of a globular flower of three petals enclosing a small ball.

Balustrade: a series of short columns, usually supporting a railing.

Bay: the space between the columns of an arcade.

Beak-head: a Norman ornamental motif, with stylised heads of birds or animals with long beaks pointing downwards, used on arches or above doorways.

Billet: a Norman ornamental motif with short raised rectangles placed at regular intervals.

Boss: a projection placed at the intersection of the ribs of a vault or roof.

Box-pew: a pew with a tall wooden enclosure.

Broach-spire: a spire at the base of which are sloping half-pyramids of stone to effect the transition from a square tower to an octagonal spire.

Buttress: a mass of masonry projecting from or built against a wall to give extra strength.

Cable-moulding: moulding resembling a twisted cord.

Camber: see *Roof.*

Capital: the top part of a pier or column.

Ceilure: an embellished part of the roof above the rood screen.

Chancel: the east end of the church in which the altar is placed.

Chancel arch: an arch at the east end of the nave opening into the chancel.

Chantry chapel: a chapel endowed for the saying of Masses for the soul(s) of the founder(s) after death.

Chapel of ease: a chapel for worshippers at some distance from the parish church.

Chevron: Norman zigzag moulding on arches or windows.

Clerestory: an upper storey of the walls of the nave pierced by windows to give additional light.

Collar-beam: see *Roof.*

Colonnade: a row of columns.

Corbel: a block of stone projecting from a wall, often supporting beams of the roof from its horizontal upper surface.

Corbel-table: a series of corbels.

Corinthian columns: one of the Orders of classical architecture.

Crocket: decorative projections on the sloping sides of spires, pinnacles, etc.

Crossing: in a cruciform church, the space at the intersection of the nave, chancel and transepts.

Cruck: see Roof.

Cupola: a domed or polygonal turret crowning a roof.

Curvilinear: see *Tracery.*

Cushion: in Norman architecture, the rounding-off of the lower angles of the capital to the circular pier below.

Dado: the lower part of the screen.

Decorated: historical division of English Gothic architecture, covering the first half of the fourteenth century.

Dogtooth: late Norman and Early English decoration consisting of a series of ornamental square pyramids.

Doom: a picture of the Last Judgment.

Dormer window: an upright window projecting from a sloping roof.

Drip-stone: see *Hood-mould.*

Early English: historical division of English Gothic architecture, covering the thirteenth century.

Easter sepulchre: a recess in the north wall of the chancel used to house the consecrated host between Maundy Thursday and Easter Day.

Fan vault: see *Vault.*

Fillet: a narrow flat band running down a shaft.

Frieze: a decorated band along the top of the tower.

Gargoyle: a stone water-spout draining a gutter, often grotesquely carved.

Geometrical: see *Tracery.*

Gothic: the style of architecture characterised by pointed arches, sub-divided into Early English, Decorated and Perpendicular.

Half-timbered: see *timber-framing.*

Hammer-beam: see *Roof.*

Herring-bone masonry: in which the component blocks are laid diagonally, alternate courses lying in opposing directions making a zigzag pattern on the face of a wall.

Hood-mould: projecting moulding over a door or window to throw off water.

Ionic columns: one of the Orders of classical architecture.

King-post: see *Roof.*

Lancet window: the tall, narrow, pointed window of the Early English period.

Light: a vertical division of a window.

Lintel: a horizontal stone over a doorway.

Long-and-short work: corner-stones placed with their long axes alternately upright and horizontal.

Misericord: a bracket on the underside of a hinged seat in the choir-stalls, providing the occupant with some support while standing.

Mullions: vertical stone bars dividing a window into 'lights'.

Nail-head: Early English ornamentation consisting of small pyramids regularly repeated.

Nimbus: a halo.

Nook-shaft: a shaft in the angle at the side of a doorway or window.

Norman architecture: the massive Romanesque style of building prevalent from 1066 to the end of the twelfth century.

Ogee arch: an arch formed by two S-shaped curves, with the concave parts above coming to a point; typical of the fourteenth century.

Order: one of the successively recessed arches of an archway; at the sides of a doorway, all the parts of a column, with base, shaft and capital.

Parclose screen: a screen separating a chapel from the rest of the church.

Pediment: a low-pitched gable, placed as a decorative feature above doorways, windows, etc.

Perpendicular; historical division of English Gothic architecture, from *c.*1350-1550.

Pier: a column of free-standing masonry supporting arches.

Pietà: a representation of the virgin Mary supporting the dead body of Jesus.

Pilaster: a shallow pier attached to a wall.

Piscina: a basin with drain on the south side of the altar for washing the vessels used during Mass.

Plate tracery: see *Tracery.*

Portico: a roof supported by columns at the entrance to a building.

Principal: see *Roof.*

Purlin: see *Roof.*

Quatrefoil: an ornament divided by cusps into four lobes.

Queen-post: see *Roof.*

Reredos: an ornamental screen or hanging on the wall behind the altar.

Respond: a half-pier carrying one end of an arch and bonded into a wall.

Reticulated tracery: see *Tracery.*

Ridge: see *Roof.*

Romanesque: an alternative name for Norman architecture, defined by round arches and vaults.

Rood: a Cross bearing the body of Jesus, flanked by the Virgin Mary and St John.

Rood-loft: a gallery on top of the rood-screen.,

Rood-screen: a screen placed at the junction of the nave and chancel, in medieval times bearing the rood.

Roof: Arched brace: inclined curved timbers strengthening collar- or hammer-beams.

  Camber: slight rise or upward curve of a horizontal structure.

  Collar-beam: a tie-beam applied higher up the slope of the roof.

  Cruck: arched beam supporting walls and roof.

  Hammer-beam: a horizontal beam projecting at the level of the wall-plate, carrying arched braces and struts.

  King-post: a central upright post connecting the tie-beam with the ridge.

  Principals: the main rafters of a roof.

  Purlins: horizontal timbers parallel with the wall-plate and the ridge-beam some way up the slope of the roof and resting on the principals.

  Queen-post: a pair of upright posts placed symmetrically on the tie-beam, connecting it with the rafters above.

  Ridge: a longitudinal beam along the angle of the roof.

  Scissor-beam: an intersecting beam placed diagonally between opposite rafters.

  Struts: beams either upright or sloping connecting king- or queen-posts to rafters above.

  Tie-beam: a horizontal timber connecting the feet of the rafters at the height of the wall-plate.

  Trussed rafters: a pair of common rafters supported by struts at their feet and tied together just below the ridge with a short, horizontal collar-beam.

  Wall-plate: a longitudinal timber laid on top of the wall.

  Wall-post: a vertical beam resting against the wall, supporting tie- or hammer-beams.

  Wind-braces: short braces connecting side purlins with principals, often decorated with cusping.

Saddleback: a tower roof shaped like a gable.

Scallop: decoration on the under surface of a capital, in which a series of truncated cones are elaborated.

Scissor-beam: see *Roof.*

Sedilia: recessed seats for priests in the south wall of the chancel.

Sheila-na-gig: a fertility figure.

Stiff-leaf: Early English type of foliage of many-lobed shapes.

String-course: a projecting line of moulding running horizontally round the walls of the church or tower.

Stoup: a receptacle for holy water placed near a door.

Strut: see *Roof.*

Tester: a canopy over the pulpit.

Three-decker pulpit: a pulpit, with clerk's stall and reading desk below.

Tie-beam: see *Roof.*

Timber-framing: a method of building where a timber framework forms the walls, the spaces filled by plaster or brick.

Tower arch: an arch usually at the west end of the nave opening into the ground floor of the tower.

Tracery: intersecting ribwork in the upper part of a window.

  Curvilinear: tracery consisting of curved lines.

  Geometrical: consisting of circles or foiled (leaf-shaped circles.)

  Plate: an early form of tracery in which openings are cut through the stone in the head of the window, often producing a Y shape.

  Reticulated: tracery in which circles are drawn at top and bottom into ogee shapes producing a net-like pattern.

Transept: transverse portion of a cross-shaped church.

Transitional: the style of building in which Gothic pointed arches exist alongside Norman architecture; typical of 1160-1200.

Transom: a horizontal bar across the opening of a window.

Trefoil: an ornament divided by cusps into three lobes.

Triptych: a set of three painted panels, hinged together.

Trussed rafters: see *Roof.*

Tuscan columns: one of the classical Orders of architecture.

Tympanum: space between the lintel of a doorway and the arch above it; sometimes applied to the space above a rood-screen.

Vault: an arched roof or ceiling.

  Fan-vault: a vault in which all the ribs springing from their origin are of the same length and curvature, and equidistant from each other.

Venetian window: a window with three openings, the central arched one wider than the others.

Volute: a spiral scroll, often found on capitals.

Wagon-roof: a roof in which closely-set rafters with arched braces gives the appearance of the inside of a covered wagon.

Wall-plate: see *Roof.*

Wall-post: see *Roof.*

Water-leaf: late Norman ornamentation in capitals, with leaves curving upwards to the angle of the abacus.

Wind-braces: see *Roof.*

Y-tracery: see *Tracery, plate.*

Bibliography and References

The basic work on Shropshire churches is *An Architectural Account of the Churches of Shropshire*, by D.H.S.Cranage, published at intervals between 1894 and 1912. This massive work is never likely to be surpassed, and I have quoted freely from it. It is not, however, a book for comfortable reading, still less for taking on a visit to Shropshire churches; my two volumes weigh 20lb!

Scarcely less useful is Nikolaus Pevsner's *Shropshire* in *The Buildings of England* series (1958, Harmondsworth), recently re-issued.

For an excellent general account of the development of English parish churches, see Richard Foster's *Discovering English Churches* (1981, London).

Richard Morris' *Churches in the Landscape* eloquently describes the evolution of parish churches in the past 1500 years (1989, London).

Other references:

Baugh, G.C. and Cox, D.C. (1981) *Monastic Shropshire*. Shrewsbury.

Ekwall, E. (1960) *The Concise Dictionary of English Place-names*. Oxford.

Gardner, A. (1940) *Alabaster Tombs of the Pre-Reformation period in England*. Cambridge.

Gethyn-Jones, E. (1979) *The Dymock School of Sculpture*. Chichester.

Jones, L.E. (1978) *The Beauty of English Churches*, London.

Klein, P. (1989) *A Guide to St Peter's Church, Stanton Lacy*. Leominster.

Klein, P. (1990) *A guide to the Heath Chapel, Shropshire*. Leominster.

Moffett, C. (1989) *Archaeological Investigations at the Anglo-Saxon Church of St Andrew, Wroxeter: 1985-6*. Trans. Shropshire Archaeological and Historical Society vol. 1xvi.

New, A. (1985) *A Guide to the Abbeys of England and Wales*. London.

Platt, C. (1976) *The English Medieval Town*. London.

Rowley, T. (1972) *The Shropshire Landscape*. London.

Salter, M. (1988) *The Old Parish Churches of Shropshire*. Wolverhampton.

Trinder, B. (1983) *A History of Shropshire*. Chichester.

Vale, E. (1949) *Shropshire* (in *The County Book Series*). London.

Vallance, A. (1936) *English Church Screens*. London.

Index